Technician Unit 11

DRAFTING FINANCIAL STATEMENTS

For assessments in December 2003
and June 2004

Assessment Kit

In this May 2003 first edition

- For assessments under the new standards
- Many additional Practice Activities
- The June and December 2002 Exams
- The AAT's Specimen Exam is included to attempt as a 'mock' under 'exam conditions'

FOR 2003 AND 2004 ASSESSMENTS

First edition May 2003

ISBN 0 7517 1143 8

British Library Cataloguing-in-Publication Data
A catalogue record for this book
is available from the British Library

Published by

BPP Professional Education
Aldine House, Aldine Place
London W12 8AW

www.bpp.com

Printed in Great Britain by W M Print
45-47 Frederick Street
Walsall, West Midlands
WS2 9NE

We are grateful to the Lead Body for Accounting for
permission to reproduce extracts from the Standards
of Competence for Accounting, and to the AAT for
permission to reproduce extracts from the mapping
and Guidance Notes.

Contents

Introduction

How to use this Assessment Kit– Unit 11 Standards of competence –
Exam Based Assessment technique – Assessment strategy

Practice activities are activities directly related to the actual content of the
BPP Interactive Text.

These are full exams providing practice for the AAT's actual exam based
assessment.

Lecturers' Resource Pack activities are activities and assessments for
lecturers to set in class or for homework. The answers are given in the BPP
Lecturers' Resource Pack.

Order form

Review form & free prize draw

Introduction

How to use this Assessment Kit

Aims of this Assessment Kit

> To provide the knowledge and practice to help you succeed in the assessment for Technician Unit 11 *Drafting Financial Statements*.

To pass the assessment successfully you need a thorough understanding in all areas covered by the standards of competence.

> To tie in with the other components of the BPP Effective Study Package to ensure you have the best possible chance of success.

Interactive Text

This covers all you need to know for the assessment for Unit 11 *Drafting Financial Statements*. Numerous activities throughout the text help you practise what you have just learnt.

Assessment Kit

When you have understood and practised the material in the Interactive Text, you will have the knowledge and experience to tackle the Assessment Kit for Unit 11 *Drafting Financial Statements*. This aims to get you through the exam. It contains past Exams for Unit 11 including the June and December 2002 Exams (amended for the new standards) and the AAT's Specimen Exam.

Passcards

These short memorable notes are focused on key topics for the Technician Units, designed to remind you of what the Interactive Text has taught you.

Recommended approach to this Assessment Kit

(a) To achieve competence in Unit 11 you need to be able to do **everything** specified by the standards. Study the Interactive Text carefully and do not skip any of it.

(b) Learning is an **active** process. Do **all** the activities as you work through the Interactive Text so you can be sure you really understand what you have read. Depending on their difficulty the activities are graded as pre-assessment or assessment.

(c) After you have covered the material in the Interactive Text, work through this **Assessment Kit**.

(d) Try the **Practice Activities**. These are linked into each chapter of the Interactive Text, and are designed to reinforce your learning and consolidate the practice that you have had doing the activities in the Interactive Text.

(e) Next do the **Exam Based Assessments**. They are designed to cover the areas you might see when you do a full exam.

(f) Finally, try the AAT's **Specimen Exam** under 'exam conditions'.

Remember this is a **practical** course.

(a) Try to relate the material to your experience in the workplace or any other work experience you may have had.

(b) Try to make as many links as you can to your study of the other units at this level.

Lecturers' Resource Pack activities

At the back of this Kit we have included a number of chapter-linked activities without answers. We have also included one full exam without answers. The answers for this section are in the BPP Lecturers' Resource Pack for this Unit.

Unit 11 Standards of competence

The structure of the Standards for Unit 11

The Unit commences with a statement of the **knowledge and understanding** which underpin competence in the Unit's elements.

The Unit of Competence is then divided into **elements of competence** describing activities which the individual should be able to perform.

Each element includes:

(a)   A set of **performance criteria.** This defines what constitutes competent performance.

(b)   A **range statement.** This defines the situations, contexts, methods etc in which competence should be displayed.

The elements of competence for Unit 11: *Drafting Financial Statements* are set out below. Knowledge and understanding required for the Unit as a whole are listed first, followed by the performance criteria and range statements for each element.

Unit 11: Drafting financial statements

What is the Unit about?

This unit is about drafting and interpreting financial statements of limited companies. The first element in this unit is about drafting limited company year-end financial statements from a trial balance. You are responsible for ensuring that the financial statements comply with any relevant domestic legislation and *either* the relevant UK standards (Statements of Standard Accounting Practice, Financial Reporting Standards and other relevant pronouncements) *or* the International Accounting Standards. You also need to show that you ensure that confidentiality procedures are followed. The second element requires you to interpret the financial statements of companies and the relationships between the elements using ratio analysis.

Elements contained within this unit are:

Element 11.1   Draft limited company financial statements
Element 11.2   Interpret limited company financial statements

Knowledge and understanding

The business environment

1 The elements and purposes of financial statements of limited companies as set out in the conceptual framework for financial reporting (Element 11.2)

2 The general legal framework of limited companies and the obligations of directors in respect of the financial statements (Element 11.1)

3 The statutory form of accounting statements and disclosure requirements (Element 11.1)

4 The UK regulatory framework for financial reporting and the main requirements of relevant Financial Reporting Standards

or

The relevant requirements of the International Accounting Standards (Element 11.1)

5 The forms of equity and loan capital (Element 11.1)

6 The presentation of corporation tax in financial statements (Element 11.1)

Accounting techniques

7 Preparing financial statements in proper form (Element 11.1)

8 Analysing and interpreting the information contained in financial statements (Element 11.2)

9 Computing and interpreting accounting ratios (Element 11.2)

Accounting principles and theory

10 Generally accepted accounting principles and concepts (Elements 11.1)

11 The general principles of consolidation (Element 11.1)

The organisation

13 How the accounting systems of an organisation are affected by its roles, organisational structure, its administrative systems and procedures and the nature of its business transactions (Elements 11.1 & 11.2)

Element 11.1 Draft limited company financial statements

Performance criteria

A   Draft **limited company financial statements** from the appropriate information

B   Correctly identify and implement subsequent adjustments and ensure that discrepancies, unusual features or queries are identified and either resolved or referred to the appropriate person

C   Ensure that **limited company financial statements** comply with **relevant accounting standards** and **domestic legislation** and with the organisation's policies, regulations and procedures

D   Prepare and interpret a limited company cash flow statement

E   Ensure that confidentiality procedures are followed at all times

Range statement

Limited company financial statements

- Income statement
- Balance sheet
- Cash flow statement (not consolidated)
- Statement of total recognised gains and losses
- The supplementary notes required by statute
- Unitary
- Consolidated

Domestic legislation

- Companies Act

Relevant accounting standards

- Relevant Statements of Standard Accounting Practice, Financial Reporting Standards and other relevant pronouncements

or

- International Accounting Standards

Element 11.2 Interpret limited company financial statements

Performance criteria

A   Identify the general purpose of financial statements used in limited companies

B   Identify the **elements** of financial statements used in limited companies

C   Identify the **relationships between the elements** within financial statements of limited companies

D   Interpret the relationship between elements of limited company financial statements using ratio analysis

E   Identify unusual features or significant issues within financial statements of limited companies

F   Draw valid conclusions from the information contained within financial statements of limited companies

G   Present issues, interpretations and conclusions clearly to the appropriate people

Range statement

Financial statements

- Balance sheet
- Income statement

Elements

- Assets
- Liabilities
- Ownership interest
- Gains
- Losses
- Contributions from owners
- Distributions to owners

Relationship between elements

- Profitability
- Liquidity
- Efficient use of resources
- Financial position

Exam Based Assessment technique

Completing exam based assessments successfully at this level is half about having the knowledge, and half about doing yourself full justice on the day. You must have the right **technique**.

The day of the exam based assessment

1 Set at least one **alarm** (or get an alarm call) for a morning exam.

2 Have **something to eat** but beware of eating too much; you may feel sleepy if your system is digesting a large meal.

3 Allow plenty of **time to get to where you are sitting the exam**; have your route worked out in advance and listen to news bulletins to check for potential travel problems.

4 **Don't forget** pens, pencils, rulers, erasers.

5 Put **new batteries** into your calculator and take a spare set (or a spare calculator).

6 **Avoid discussion** about the exam assessment with other candidates outside the venue.

Technique in the exam based assessment

1 **Read the instructions (the 'rubric') on the front of the assessment carefully**

Check that the format hasn't changed. It is surprising how often assessors' reports remark on the number of students who do not attempt all the tasks.

2 **Read the paper twice**

Read through the paper twice – don't forget that you are given 15 minutes' reading time. Check carefully that you have got the right end of the stick before putting pen to paper. Use your 15 minutes' reading time wisely. **From June 2003**, reading time can only be used for **reading**. You may not make notes or use a calculator during those 15 minutes.

3 **Check the time allocation for each section of the exam**

Time allocations are given for each section of the exam. When the time for a section is up, you should go on to the next section.

4 **Read the task carefully and plan your answer**

Read through the task again very carefully when you come to answer it. Plan your answer to ensure that you **keep to the point**. Two minutes of planning plus eight minutes of writing is virtually certain to produce a better answer than ten minutes of writing. Planning will also help you answer the assessment efficiently, for example by identifying workings that can be used for more than one task.

5 **Produce relevant answers**

Particularly with written answers, make sure you **answer what has been set**, and not what you would have preferred to have been set. Do not, for example, answer a question on **why** something is done with an explanation of **how** it is done.

6 **Work your way steadily through the exam**

Don't get bogged down in one task. If you are having problems with something, the chances are that everyone else is too.

7 **Produce an answer in the correct format**

The assessor will state **in the requirements** the format which should be used, for example in a report or memorandum.

8 **Do what the assessor wants**

You should ask yourself what the assessor is expecting in an answer; many tasks will demand a combination of technical knowledge and business commonsense. Be careful if you are required to give a decision or make a recommendation; you cannot just list the criteria you will use, but you will also have to say whether those criteria have been fulfilled.

9 **Lay out your numerical computations and use workings correctly**

Make sure the layout is in a style the assessor likes.

Show all your **workings** clearly and explain what they mean. Cross reference them to your answer. This will help the assessor to follow your method (this is of particular importance where there may be several possible answers).

10 **Present a tidy paper**

You are a professional, and it should show in the **presentation of your work**. You should make sure that you write legibly, label diagrams clearly and lay out your work neatly.

11 **Stay until the end of the exam**

Use any spare time **checking and rechecking** your script. Check that you have answered all the requirements of the task and that you have clearly labelled your work. Consider also whether your answer appears reasonable in the light of the information given in the question.

12 **Don't worry if you feel you have performed badly in the exam**

It is more than likely that the other candidates will have found the assessment difficult too. As soon as you get up to leave the venue, **forget** that assessment and think about the next – or, if it is the last one, celebrate!

13 **Don't discuss an exam with other candidates**

This is particularly the case if you **still have other exams to sit**. Even if you have finished, you should put it out of your mind until the day of the results. Forget about exams and relax!

Assessment strategy

This Unit is assessed by **exam based assessment** only.

Exam based assessment

An exam based assessment is a means of collecting evidence that you have the **essential knowledge and understanding** which underpins competence. It is also a means of collecting evidence across the **range of contexts** for the standards, and of your ability to **transfer skills**, knowledge and understanding to different situations. Thus, although central assessments contain practical tests linked to the performance criteria, they also focus on the underpinning knowledge and understanding. You should, in addition, expect each central assessment to contain tasks taken from across a broad range of the standards.

Format of exam

There will be a three hour exam in two sections.

Section 1:   Element 11.1 (70% of the assessment)
Section 2:   Element 11.2 (30% of the assessment)

There will be an additional 15 minutes reading time.

Guidance on the time allocation of tasks will be given in the exam.

The tasks are generally of a practical nature, designed to provide evidence that the performance criteria have been met and to ensure that the relevant knowledge and understanding is present.

Further guidance

The Standard is divided into two elements. Element 11.1 is called 'Draft limited company financial statements' and Element 11.2 is called 'Interpret limited company financial statements'.

Element 11.1 requires that the financial statements be drafted from appropriate information. This might include:

- A trial balance or an extended trial balance
- Other information about balances or transactions relating to the period under consideration

Students may be asked to draft financial statements for single companies or consolidated group accounts. Performance Criteria D makes it clear that the drafting of cash flow statements is also included in this Element. These may be drafted from the other financial statements of a company in conjunction with further relevant information.

In drafting financial statements the knowledge and understanding required is set out in the Standards. Students will need to know and understand the general legal framework of limited companies and the obligations of directors in respect of the financial statements. This includes a grasp of the Companies Act accounting and reporting requirements. The student must thus be aware of the statutory form of accounting statements and disclosure requirements in order that they can prepare the financial statements in proper form. This includes an understanding of the content and form of published accounts of limited companies. The Companies Act Format 1 for profit and loss accounts and balance sheets are used in the pro-formas provided in Central Assessments. Items required to be disclosed in notes to the accounts by the Companies Act Schedule 4 Part III, the disclosure of Directors' emoluments under Schedule 6 Part I and the requirements for disclosure of auditor's remuneration under Section 390A of the Companies Act must be grasped. The additional requirements of FRS 3 for profit and loss accounts and STRGL must also be understood and applied where required. Cash flow statements are to be drafted in accordance with the requirements of FRS 1 (Revised).

There must be an understanding of the UK regulatory framework of financial reporting. This includes a grasp of which bodies are involved in the standard-setting process, the process by which standards are promulgated, the structure of regulation and the roles of the bodies involved and the process of enforcing standards. Drafting financial statements involves a grasp of generally accepted accounting principles and concepts as well as detailed knowledge of the main requirements of relevant Statements of Standard Accounting Practice, Financial Reporting Standards and other relevant pronouncements or, where applicable, the requirements of relevant International Accounting Standards (IAS) (from December 2004 only).

Drafting consolidated financial statements involves as grasp of the general principles of consolidation. Only simple consolidations will be assessed. This will involve minority interests and pre-acquisition profits. However, the consolidation of sub-subsidiaries or acquisitions where shares in subsidiary undertakings are acquired at different times will not be assessable. Simple equity accounting form associated companies is assessable. The forms of equity and loan capital and the presentation of corporation tax in financial statements must be understood for all companies.

Performance criteria for Element 11.2

This element requires students to understand the general purposes of limited company financial statements. The Range Statement makes clear that the financial statements in question are the balance sheet and income statement. The objective of financial statements is set out in Chapter 1 of the UK's conceptual framework The *Statement of Principles for Financial Reporting* (SOP). A knowledge of the purposes of financial statements as set out in this document is required by the knowledge and understanding of this Unit. The users of financial statements and the purposes for which they use financial statements are set out in the SOP.

The elements of financial statements are set out in the Range Statement. This follows the identification of elements given in the SOP. The elements are assets, liabilities, ownership interest, gains, losses, contributions from owners and distributions to owners and each of these are explained in the SOP. Students need to understand how these elements relate to each other within financial statements. This involves a grasp of which financial statement they appear in and how they are related to each other within the statements. In the balance sheet the relationship between assets, liabilities and ownership interest need to be understood using the accounting equation. The effect of contributions from owners and distributions to owners on the balance of ownership interest needs to be grasped. How gains and losses are reflected in the income statement must be understood and how the income statement articulates with the balance sheet must be grasped.

Students must also be able to interpret the relationship between elements of limited company financial statements using ratio analysis. This involves computing and interpreting accounting ratios relating to profitability, liquidity, efficient use of resources and financial position. Unusual features or significant issues raised by the analysis should be identified. Valid conclusions should be drawn from this information and the issues, interpretations and conclusions should be clearly presented to appropriate people.

Typical tasks in the first section

- Preparing a consolidated profit and loss account for a limited company

- Preparing a consolidated balance sheet for a limited company

- Calculating the goodwill on acquisition and/or minority interest for a limited company

- Calculating the amount at which an interest in an associate is to be included in consolidated financial statements

- Making adjustments to the balances in a trial balance or extended trial balance of a company in accordance with the requirements of company law, accounting concepts and accounting standards

- Explaining the UK regulatory framework of financial reporting including the bodies involved and their respective roles

- Explaining the reason for the adjustments by reference to company law, accounting concepts and accounting standards

- Drafting a profit and loss account and/or a balance sheet from a trial balance or extended trial balance in accordance with the format and requirements of company law and accounting standards

- Explaining the requirements for the accounting treatment of items in company financial statements by reference to the requirements of accounting standards

- Drafting notes to the accounts as required by company law and accounting standards

- Explaining the general legal framework of limited companies and the obligations of directors in respect of the financial statements

- Drafting a reconciliation of movements in shareholders' funds and a note of historical cost profits and losses for a limited company

- Drafting a statement of total recognised gains and losses for a limited company

- Drafting a cash flow statement and/or a reconciliation between operating profit and cash flow from operating activities from the financial statements of a limited company

- Interpreting a cash flow statement

Typical tasks in the second section

- Setting out the general purposes of financial statements and illustrating these in relation to users and their needs

- Identifying and explaining the elements of financial statements

- Explaining what is meant by the balance sheet equation and how the elements fit into the equation

- Explaining the articulation of the balance sheet with the profit and loss account and STRGL

- Demonstrating the effect of contributions from owners and distributions to owners on ownership interest

- Calculating ratios for limited companies

- Interpreting the meaning of the ratios and of changes in the ratios of limited companies

- Comparing ratios of limited companies with industry averages

- Setting out the results of the computation and analysis of ratios in report format or in a letter and clearly setting out conclusions of the analysis therein

What is the Chief Assessor looking for?

What is expected of competent students in this Unit and some typical areas of weakness are set out below.

Section 1

(a) Students need to have a clear grasp what is involved in drafting consolidated financial statements. This involves a clear understanding of when there is a parent/subsidiary undertaking relationship. The student must grasp the principles behind consolidated accounts and demonstrate a clear grasp of the techniques of producing consolidated profit and loss accounts and balance sheets. The lack of a clear technique often lies behind the failure to demonstrate competence in these tasks.

(b) In order to show competence in the tasks of adjusting balances a clear grasp of the accounts affected by transactions or the requirements of company law, accounting concepts and accounting standards is required as well as a grasp of the mechanics of journal entries. Failure in this area would result from a lack of precision in identifying the accounts affected and through confusions as to when an account is debited or credited.

(c)   Students need to be able to draft financial statements in accordance with the requirements of the Companies Act and accounting standards. This involves an ability to enter the balances and transactions correctly onto the pro-formas provided. Students who are not sufficiently familiar with the accounts that form part of the financial statement balances may encounter problems. The lack of knowledge of certain accounting standards undermines efforts to answer the tasks that require an explanation of adjustments to account balances or an explanation of accounting treatment of certain items in the financial statements of companies.

(d)   The drafting of financial statements in accordance with FRS 3, including the STRGL, may have caused problems for students. An adequate familiarity with the requirements of this accounting standard is required.

(e)   Tasks which require the drafting of notes to the accounts may suffer from an occasional gap in knowledge. Once again, reference to the guidance given by the AAT on the assessable notes should be made to ensue adequate coverage.

(f)   Knowledge of the standard-setting process and the bodies involved in the promulgation and policing of accounting standards is required by the Unit. A lack of precise knowledge of the bodies involved and their particular roles may result in a lack of competence in tasks in this area.

(g)   The drafting of cash flow statements and the reconciliation and notes required by FRS 1 (Revised) is required by this Unit. A clear grasp of the technique of drafting such a statement and reconciliation may prove problematic for some students. The interpretation of such statements may also present particular problems for students. It is important to try and relate the information presented in cash flow statements into a coherent whole. Part of the problem with such tasks is the potential failure of students to be explicit in stating what information the cash flow statement and the reconciliation are giving about the company. Figures may be left to speak for themselves and hence there would appear to be little in the way of interpretation of the information.

Section 2

(a)   Students must demonstrate an awareness of the overall purpose of financial statements and of the particular purposes of individual users of financial statements. Students may not be competent on these tasks because they do not pay sufficient attention to the requirements of the task. Students need to be able to distinguish external and internal users of financial information as well as appreciating the difference between the use of financial statements for the purposes of stewardship and other economic decisions.

(b)   The student must be able to identify the elements of financial statements and give appropriate definitions. Some students may not be competent because they do not set out definitions of the elements with sufficient precision. They might fail to adequately explain the elements in terms of the SOP definitions and give examples of elements rather than explanations of the sort of thing that they are.

(c)   Student must have a clear grasp of the accounting equation and be able to show how the equation reflects the equation through a numerical example. The articulation of the profit and loss account with the balance sheet needs to be grasped and students should be prepared to show how the profit for the year and any other gains shown in the STRGL changes the ownership interest.

(d)   The calculation of the various ratios that show profitability, liquidity, efficient use of resources and financial position is required by the Unit. This involves a grasp of the formulas. In general, students must demonstrate a grasp of the meaning of the ratios, the import of changes in the ratios from one year to the next or of the differences in ratios between two companies and/or the industry averages. The results of the analysis should be clearly set out and relevant conclusions drawn. Students may not demonstrate competence because their analysis is superficial and does not demonstrate a clear understanding of the ratios and the information they convey. Sometimes the ratios may be left to speak for themselves and little more is said than that the ratio went up or down without any indication of the effect that this has on the company. Conclusions may be inadequately supported or not derived from a consideration of the preceding analysis. The presentation of answers to some of the tasks may not be in accordance with the requirements of the task. Credit for presentation would be accordingly lost.

Practice
Activities

BPP
PROFESSIONAL EDUCATION

chapters 1 and 2

Introduction; Accounting conventions

1 Objectives

(a)   State the objectives of financial reporting.

(b)   Identify the various groups of users of a financial reporting package.

(c)   Discuss the information needs of any two of the groups of users identified above.

(d)   Discuss the following statement: 'The diverse information needs of the various user groups cannot be fully met by the current financial reporting package used by companies?'.   **(20 mins)**

2 Accounting equation

The accounting equation of a business is as follows:

Assets £1,200 – Liabilities £800 = Ownership interest £400

The business subsequently makes two transactions.

1   It purchases on credit stock costing £120.
2   It sells the stock purchased in (1) for £180 cash.

Tasks

(a)   Explain what is meant by 'assets', 'liabilities' and 'ownership interest'.

(b)   Explain the effect of each transaction on the elements in the balance sheet.

(c)   State the accounting equation for the business after the two transactions have taken place.

(d)   Draft a simple profit and loss account for the two transactions.

(e)   Give an example of a user who might be interested in a profit and loss account. Explain how the user you have chosen might find the statement useful.

(25 mins)

3 Objective and elements

(a)   What is the objective of financial statements?

(b)   Illustrate how this objective is fulfilled by considering the financial statements of limited companies and one type of public sector or not-for-profit organisation.

(c)   Identify the elements of financial statements.

(d)   Explain how the elements are related in the balance sheet and in the profit and loss account of a company and the relationship between the two financial statements.

(20 mins)

4 Assets and liabilities

(a)   Why is plant and machinery included in the fixed assets of a company classified as an 'asset' of the business?

(b)   Why is a bank loan classified as a 'liability' of the business?

(c)   (i)   Why is the final figure of 'retained profit for the year' in the profit and loss account not the same figure that appears in the balance for the profit and loss account on the balance sheet of the company?

       (ii)   Is there any connection between the two figures?

(20 mins)

PROFESSIONAL EDUCATION

5 Balancing

(a) How can the accounting equation in a company balance?

(b) Give two examples of users outside a company, other than the shareholders, who may be interested in its financial statements. For each user, state what purpose they would use them for.

(20 mins)

chapters 3 and 4

Regulation

6 Accounting standards

Which regulatory bodies are involved in the process of setting and enforcing accounting standards in the United Kingdom? Give a brief description of their roles.

(20 mins)

chapters 5 to 7

Fixed assets
and stocks

Activity checklist

This checklist shows which performance criteria, range statement or knowledge and understanding point is covered by each activity in this chapter. Tick off each activity as you complete it.

Activity

7		Performance Criteria 11.2.C: ensure that limited company financial statements comply with relevant accounting standards
8		Performance Criteria 11.2.C: ensure that limited company financial statements comply with relevant accounting standards
9		Performance Criteria 11.2.C: ensure that limited company financial statements comply with relevant accounting standards
10		Performance Criteria 11.2.C: ensure that limited company financial statements comply with relevant accounting standards
11		Performance Criteria 11.2.C: ensure that limited company financial statements comply with relevant accounting standards

7 Depreciation

Explain briefly the provisions of FRS 15 *Tangible fixed assets* where:

(a)   An asset is disposed of
(b)   The method of depreciating assets is changed

Guidance notes

1   In part (a) you should try to think carefully whether the provisions of the FRS 3 have any relevance here.

2   Part (b) is more difficult to explain in words than to apply in practice!

8 Revaluations

Prepare brief notes to take to a Board meeting covering the following questions of the directors.

(a)   If we decide to adopt a policy of revaluation of land and buildings, do we need to revalue all the land and buildings that we own or can some continue to be shown at historical cost?

(b)   If we do revalue land and buildings:

    (i)   What should be the carrying value at the balance sheet date?

    (ii)   What valuation basis should we adopt for our land and buildings given that they are non-specialised properties?

    (iii)   Where should we recognise any gain that is made on revaluation.

Explain your answers by reference to relevant accounting standards.

(15 mins)

9 Stocks

SSAP 9 *Stocks and long-term contracts* states that stocks and work in progress, other than long-term contract work in progress, should be valued at the 'lower of cost and net realisable value'. You are required to define the meaning of:

(a)   Cost
(b)   Net realisable value

Guidance notes

1   A very straightforward question, particularly if you have a good memory!

2   You should know these definitions very well as you will almost certainly be asked to apply them to a practical problem.

3   A 'memory test' such as this may well come up as part of a longer task. It is an easy way of demonstrating your competence, and you would be advised to do it first to give yourself confidence.

10 SSAP 13

SSAP 13 *Accounting for research and development* defines certain categories of research and development expenditure. The standard also lays down rules which must be applied to the capitalisation of research and development expenditure.

Tasks

(a)   List and explain the categories of expenditure.   (10 mins)

(b)   Explain the criteria applied to research and development expenditure, according to SSAP 13, to determine whether the cost should be capitalised.   (27 mins)

(c)   Discuss briefly why there was a need for a SSAP relating to research and development expenditure.

        (13 mins)

(50 mins)

11 Goodwill

What are the options available for the accounting treatment of goodwill arising on acquisition in group accounts?

(15 mins)

chapter 8

Reporting financial performance

Activity checklist

This checklist shows which performance criteria, range statement or knowledge and understanding point is covered by each activity in this chapter. Tick off each activity as you complete it.

Activity

12	☐	Range Statement for 11.1: Statement of total recognised gains and losses

12 Jenny

You are provided with the following data, relating to Jenny Ltd for the year ended 31 March 20X1.

(a) Jenny Ltd's profit for the financial year was £1,145,000
(b) Land was revalued at market value of £1,500,000. Its book value had been £1,000,000.

Tasks

(a) Prepare a statement of total recognised gains and losses for Jenny Ltd for the year ended 31 March 20X1.

(b) FRS 3 *Reporting financial performance* requires separate disclosure of the results of continuing operations, acquisitions and discontinued operations.

Prepare notes to explain:

(i) What is meant, in FRS 3, by 'acquisitions' and 'discontinued operations'

(ii) Why it is useful to distinguish between the three types of operations for the purposes of financial reporting?

(20 mins)

chapters 3 to 9

Limited company scenario questions

Activity checklist

This checklist shows which performance criteria, range statement or knowledge and understanding point is covered by each activity in this chapter. Tick off each activity as you complete it.

Activity

13		Performance Criteria 11.1A, B and C
14		Performance Criteria 11.1A, B and C
15		Performance Criteria 11.1A, B and C
17		Performance Criteria 11.1A, B and C
18		Performance Criteria 11.1A, B and C
19		Performance Criteria 11.1A, B and C
20		Performance Criteria 11.1A, B and C
21		Performance Criteria 11.1A, B and C
22		Performance Criteria 11.1A, B and C

13 Fun

You have been asked to assist in the preparation of the financial statements of Fun Ltd for the year ended 30 September 20X8. The company is a distributor of children's games. You have been provided with the extended trial balance of Fun Ltd as at 30 September 20X8, which is set out on page 16.

You have been given the following further information.

(a) The share capital of the business consists of ordinary shares with a nominal value of 25 pence.

(b) The company has paid an interim dividend of 6 pence per share this year and is proposing a final dividend of 10 pence per share.

(c) Depreciation has been calculated on all of the fixed assets of the business and has already been entered into the distribution costs and administrative expenses ledger balances as shown on the extended trial balance.

(d) The corporation tax charge for the year has been calculated as £972,000.

(e) Interest on the loan has been paid for the first eleven months of the year only, but no interest has been paid or charged for the final month of the year. The loan carries a rate of interest of 8% per annum of the balance outstanding on the loan.

Tasks

(a) Make any additional adjustments you feel to be necessary to the balances in the extended trial balance as a result of the matters set out in the further information above. Set out your adjustments in the form of journal entries.

Notes

1 Narratives and dates are not required.
2 Ignore any effect of these adjustments on the tax charge for the year as given above.

(b) Taking account of any adjustments made in Part (a), draft a profit and loss account for the year ended 30 September 20X8 using Format 1 in accordance with the Companies Act 1985 as supplemented by FRS 3 *Reporting financial performance*.

You are *not* required to produce note to the accounts.

(c) The directors are interested in expanding operations next year. They wish to be clear about the constituents of the equity on the balance sheet and on the impact that leasing equipment, rather than purchasing equipment, might have on the company's balance sheet. They would like you to attend the next meeting of the Board.

Prepare notes to bring to the Board meeting dealing with the following matters.

(i) How the balances on the share premium and the revaluation reserve arose.

(ii) The recommendation of one of the directors is to lease the assets as he says that this means that the asset can be kept off the balance sheet. Comment on this recommendation.

(50 mins)

FUN LIMITED
EXTENDED TRIAL BALANCE AS AT 30 SEPTEMBER 20X8

	Trial balance		Adjustments		Profit and loss account		Balance sheet	
	Debit £'000	Credit £'000	Debit £'000	Credit £'000	Debit £'000	Credit £'000	Debit £'000	Credit £'000
Trade debtors	2,863						2,863	
Bank overdraft		316						316
Interest	300				300			
Profit and loss account		3,811						3,811
Provision for doubtful debts		114						114
Distribution costs	2,055		614		2,669			
Administrative expenses	1,684		358		2,042			
Returns inwards	232				232			
Sales		14,595				14,595		
Land – cost	2,293						2,293	
Buildings – cost	2,857						2,857	
Fixtures and fittings – cost	1,245						1,245	
Motor vechicles – cost	2,524						2,524	
Office equipment – cost	872						872	
Stock	1,893		2,041	2,041	1,893	2,041	2,041	
Purchases	6,671				6,671			
Interim dividend	480				480			
Trade creditors		804						804
Buildings – accumulated depreciation		261		51				312
Fixtures and fittings – accumulated depreciation		309		124				433
Motor vehicles – accumulated depreciation		573		603				1,176
Office equipment – accumulated depreciation		184		81				265
Prepayments	63						63	
Carriage inwards	87				87			
Returns outwards		146				146		
Accruals				113				113
Investments	2,244						2,244	
Loan		3,600						3,600
Ordinary share capital		2,000						2,000
Share premium		1,300						1,300
Revaluation reserve		350						350
Profit					2,408			2,408
TOTAL	28,363	28,363	3,013	3,013	16,782	16,782	17,002	17,002

14 Franco

You are employed by a firm of certified accountants and have been asked to prepare the financial statements of Franco Ltd (a company which distributes confectionery) for the year ending 31 March 20X5. A bookkeeper at the company has prepared an extended trial balance for the year ending 31 March 20X5; this includes the normal year-end adjustments. You have been asked to review the trial balance in the light of some further information which may be relevant to the accounts and to make any adjustments necessary before they are published.

The extended trial balance of Franco Ltd is set out on page 18.

The following further information is provided.

(a)   The corporation tax charge for the year has been agreed at £110,000.

(b)   Motor expenses of £10,000 and wages of £2,000 have been wrongly included in the general expenses figure in the trial balance. Of the remaining general expenses, £100,000 should be classified as administrative, the balance being distribution expenses.

(c)   The amount representing share capital and reserves in the extended trial balance consists of 400,000 50p ordinary shares and 50,000 £1 (8%) preference shares. The directors have just declared the final dividend for the ordinary shares and this has not yet been entered into the accounts. The preference dividend also needs to be provided for. The total (ordinary and preference) dividend for the year amounts to £72,000.

(d)   Interest due on the long-term loan for the year needs to be provided for; it is charged at 10% per annum.

(e)   An audit fee of £9,000 needs to be provided for.

(f)   Included in the total salaries figure is £98,000 of directors' emoluments. £68,000 of directors' emoluments should be classed as administrative expenses, the remainder being distribution. £104,000 of salaries and wages (excluding directors' emoluments) should be classed as administrative expenses, the remainder being distribution expenses.

(g)   Rates and light and heat should be split equally between administration and distribution expenses.

(h)   £27,000 of motor expenses are to be classed as distribution, the remainder as administration expenses.

(i)   The depreciation charges should be classed as:

	Administration £	Distribution £
Buildings	3,000	1,000
Fixtures and fittings	4,000	1,000
Motor vehicles	2,000	8,000
Office equipment	1,000	−

(j)   The insurance payment should be split in the ratio of 75/25 between administration and distribution expenses respectively.

FRANCO LIMITED
EXTENDED TRIAL BALANCE AS AT 31 MARCH 20X5

Folio	Description	Ledger balances DR £'000	Ledger balances CR £'000	Adjustments DR £'000	Adjustments CR £'000	Profit & Loss Account DR £'000	Profit & Loss Account CR £'000	Balance Sheet Balances DR £'000	Balance Sheet Balances CR £'000
	Turnover		2,470				2,470		
	Purchases	1,000				1,000			
	Salaries and wages	400				400			
	Motor expenses	27				27			
	Rates	25			5	20			
	Light and heat	32		4		36			
	Carriage inwards	14				14			
	Advertising	95				95			
	Stock	215		225	225	215	225	225	
	Trade debtors	450						450	
	Provision for doubtful debts		6		3				9
	Increase in prov for doubtful debts			3		3			
	Cash in hand	1						1	
	Cash at bank	6						6	
	Trade creditors		170						170
	Land (cost)	375						375	
	Buildings (cost)	200						200	
	Fixtures and fittings (cost)	35						35	
	Motor vehicles (cost)	94						94	
	Office equipment (cost)	20						20	
	Buildings (acc dep)		20		4				24
	Fixtures and fittings (acc dep)		18		5				23
	Motor vehicles (acc dep)		54		10				64
	Office equipment (acc dep)		4		1				5
	Depreciation - buildings			4		4			
	Depreciation - fixtures and fittings			5		5			
	Depreciation - motor vehicles			10		10			
	Depreciation - office equipment			1		1			
	Returns inwards	10				10			
	Interim dividend	30				30			
	Returns outwards		5				5		
	General expenses	135				135			
	Insurance	13			1	12			
	Profit and loss account		160						160
	Accruals				4				4
	Prepayment			6				6	
	Share capital - ordinary shares		200						200
	- preference shares		50						50
	Long term loan		20						20
	Profit					683			683
		3,177	3,177	258	258	2,700	2,700	1,412	1,412

Tasks

(a)   Make any adjustments you feel necessary to the balances in the extended trial balance as a result of the matters set out in the further information on pages 28 and 31. Set out your adjustments in the form of journal entries. (Ignore the effect of any adjustments on the tax charge for the year.

(b)   Draft a profit and loss account for the year ended 31 March 20X5 and a balance sheet as at that date in a form suitable for publication using Format 1 in accordance with the Companies Act as supplemented by FRS 3 *Reporting financial performance*. (You are *not* required to prepare a statement of total recognised gains and losses or the reconciliation of movements in shareholders' funds required under FRS 3.)

(c)   You have been asked by the directors of the company to prepare a short report covering the following.

   (i)   Stock is valued at the lower of cost and net realisable value in the accounts in accordance with SSAP 9. The directors would like you to explain how cost and net realisable value are derived.

   (ii)   The directors have heard of the filing exemptions available to small companies, and they would like you to explain what these exemptions are.

   Write a report which covers the required points.

(d)   The Directors of Franco Ltd have drawn your attention to three matters and requested your advice on how these should be treated.

   (i)   An issue of shares was made on 10 April 20X5. Fifty thousand 50p ordinary shares were issued at a premium of 25p.

   (ii)   A debtor owing £30,000 to Franco Ltd on 31 March 20X5 went into liquidation on 3 April 20X5. The £30,000 is still unpaid and it is unclear whether any monies will be received.

   (iii)   The company is awaiting the outcome of a legal suit; an independent lawyer has assessed that it is probable that the company will gain £25,000 from it.

   Write a memo to the directors of Franco Ltd outlining the required treatment for *each* of the three events.

(e)   Financial statements should be prepared on the basis of conditions which exist at the balance sheet date. The term 'window dressing' is used to describe a situation where transactions have been undertaken just before the balance sheet date and will be reversed after that date, simply to improve the appearance of the position of the company at the year end.

   (i)   Give two examples of how window dressing may be used to improve the cash balance in the balance sheet.

   (i)   Explain how SSAP 17 *Post balance sheet events* requires window dressing to be dealt with.

(105 mins)

15 Dowango

You have been assigned to assist in the preparation of the financial statements of Dowango Ltd for the year ended 31 March 20X6. The company is a cash and carry operation that trades from a large warehouse on an industrial estate. You have been provided with the extended trial balance of Dowango Ltd on 31 March 20X6 which is set out on page 21.

You have been given the following further information.

(a) The authorised and issued share capital of the business consists of ordinary shares with a nominal value of £1.

(b) The company has paid an interim dividend of 4p per share during the year but has not provided for the final dividend of 6p per share.

(c) Depreciation has been calculated on all of the fixed assets of the business and has already been entered on a monthly basis into the distribution expenses and administration costs ledger balances as shown on the extended trial balance.

(d) The tax charge for the year has been calculated as £211,000.

(e) Interest on the long-term loan has been paid for six months of the year. No adjustment has been made for the interest due for the final six months of the year. Interest is charged on the loan at a rate of 10% per annum.

(f) An advertising campaign was undertaken during the year at a cost of £19,000. No invoices have yet been received for this campaign and no adjustment for this expense has been made in the extended trial balance.

(g) The investments consist of shares in a retail company that were purchased with a view to resale at a profit. Dowango Ltd own 2% of the share capital of the company. At the end of the year a valuation of the shares was obtained with a view to selling the shares in the forthcoming year. The shares were valued at £56,000.

Tasks

(a) Make any adjustments you feel to be necessary to the balances in the extended trial balance as a result of the matters set out in the further information above. Set out your adjustments in the form of journal entries. Narratives are not required. (Ignore any effect of these adjustments on the tax charge for the year as given above.)

(b) Draft a profit and loss account for the year ended 31 March 20X6 and a balance sheet as at that date using Format 1 in accordance with the Companies Act 1985 as supplemented by FRS 3 *Reporting financial performance.*

(Your are *not* required to prepare a statement of total recognised gains and losses or the reconciliation of movements in shareholders' funds required under FRS 3.)

DOWANGO LIMITED: EXTENDED TRIAL BALANCE AS AT 31 MARCH 20X6

Description	Trial balance		Adjustments		Profit and loss a/c		Balance sheet	
	Debit £'000	Credit £'000	Debit £'000	Credit £'000	Debit £'000	Credit £'000	Debit £'000	Credit £'000
Land (cost)	431						431	
Buildings (cost)	512						512	
Fixtures & fittings (cost)	389						389	
Motor vehicles (cost)	341						341	
Office equipment - (cost)	105						105	
Buildings - (accumulated depreciation)		184						184
Fixtures & fittings - (accumulated depreciation)		181						181
Motor vehicles - (accumulated depreciation)		204						204
Office equipment - (accumulated depreciation)		56						56
Stock	298		365	365	298	365	365	
Investments	64						64	
Debtors	619						619	
Provision for doubtful debts		27						27
Prepayments			21				21	
Cash in hand	3						3	
Cash at bank		157						157
Creditors		331						331
Accruals				41				41
Sales		5,391				5,391		
Purchases	2,988				2,988			
Returns inwards	39				39			
Returns outwards		31				31		
Carriage inwards	20				20			
Distribution expenses	1,092		23	11	1,104			
Administrative costs	701		18	10	709			
Interest charges	15				15			
Interim dividend	20				20			
Share capital		500						500
Profit and loss account		275						275
Long term loan		300						300
Profit					594			594
	7,637	7,637	427	427	5,787	5,787	2,850	2,850

(c)   The directors of Dowango Ltd have asked to have a meeting with you. They are intending to ask the bank for a further long-term loan to enable them to purchase a company which has retail outlets. The directors have identified two possible companies to take over and they intend to purchase the whole of the share capital of one of the two targeted companies. The directors have obtained the latest financial statements of the two companies in summary form, and have also sent you a letter with some questions that they would like you to answer. The financial statements and the letter are set out below and on page 35.

SUMMARY PROFIT AND LOSS ACCOUNTS

	Company A	Company B
	£'000	£'000
Turnover	800	2,100
Cost of sales	440	1,050
Gross profit	360	1,050
Expenses	160	630
Net profit before interest and tax	200	420

SUMMARY BALANCE SHEETS

	Company A	Company B
	£'000	£'000
Fixed assets	620	1,640
Net current assets	380	1,160
Long-term loan	(400)	(1,100)
	600	1,700
Share capital and reserves	600	1,700

DOWANGO LTD

Dear AAT student

In preparation for discussions about a possible loan to Dowango Ltd, the bank has asked to see the latest financial statements of Dowango Ltd. We wish to ensure that the financial statements show the company in the best light. In particular, we wish to ensure that the assets of the business are shown at their proper value. We would like to discuss with you the following issues.

(a)   The fixed assets of our company are undervalued. We have received a professional valuation of the land and buildings which shows that they are worth more than is stated in our financial statements. The land has a current market value of £641,000 and the buildings are valued at £558,000.

(b)   The investments are recorded in our trial balance at cost. We realise that the market value of the investments is less than the cost, but since we have not yet sold them, we have not made a loss on it and so we should continue to show them at cost.

(c)   Stocks are recorded in our balance sheet at cost. Most of our stock is worth more than this as we could sell it for more than we paid for it. Only a few items would sell for less than we paid for them. We have worked out the real value of our stock as follows.

	Cost	Sales prices
	£'000	£'000
Undervalued items	340	460
Overvalued items	25	15
Total	365	475

We have set out a number of questions we would like answered at our meeting in an appendix to this letter. We would also like you to advise us at that meeting on the profitability and return on capital of the two companies targeted for takeover (whose financial statements we have already sent to you) and on the reporting implications if we purchase one of the companies.

Yours sincerely

The directors

(i) The questions from the appendix to the directors' letter are shown below. Write a memo to the directors answering these questions, which relate to the financial statements of Dowango Ltd. Explain your answers, where relevant, by reference to company law, accounting concepts and applicable accounting standards.

(1) Can we show the land and buildings at valuation rather than cost?

(2) If we did so, how would the valuation of land and buildings be reflected in the financial statements?

(3) Would revaluing the land and buildings have any effect upon the gearing ratio of the company and would this assist us in our attempt to get a loan from the bank?

(4) What effect would a revaluation have upon the future results of the company?

(ii) Can we continue to show the investments at cost?

(iii) What is the best value for stock that we can show in our balance sheet in the light of the information we have given you about sales price?

(d) Advise the directors as to which of the two companies targeted for takeover is the more profitable and which one provides the higher return on capital. Your answer should include calculation of the following ratios.

(i) Return on capital employed
(ii) Net profit margin
(iii) Asset turnover

You should also calculate and comment on at least one further ratio of your choice, for which you have sufficient information, which would be relevant to determining which of the companies is more profitable or provides the greater return on capital.

(e) Advise the directors as to whether Dowango Ltd would have any further reporting requirements in the future as a result of the purchase of shares in one of the companies targeted for takeover.

(54 mins)

16 Primavera Fashions

You have been assigned to assist in the preparation of the financial statements of Primavera Fashions Ltd for the year ended 31 March 20X7. The company is a trading company which distributes fashion clothing. It has one subsidiary undertaking and one associated company.

Primavera Fashions Ltd recently engaged a financial accountant to manage a team of book-keepers. The book-keepers produced a correct extended trial balance of the company and gave it to the accountant so that he could draft the year end financial statements.

The book-keeping staff have reported that he appeared to have some difficulty with the task and, after several days, apparently gave up the task and has not been seen since. He left behind him a balance sheet and some pages of workings which appear to contain a number of errors.

There is to be a meeting of the Board next week at which the financial statements will be approved. You have been brought in to assist in the production of a corrected balance sheet and to advise the directors on matters concerning the year end accounts. The uncorrected balance sheet, the workings left by the financial accountant and the correct extended trial balance of Primavera Fashions Ltd on 31 March 20X7 are set out on the following pages.

PRIMAVERA FASHIONS LIMITED
BALANCE SHEET AS AT 31 MARCH 20X7

	£'000	£'000
Fixed assets		
Intangible assets		128
Tangible assets		3,948
Investments		2,924
		7,000
Current assets		
Stocks	1,097	
Debtors	924	
Cash at bank and in hand	152	
	2,173	
Creditors: amounts falling due within one year	2,486	
Net current assets (liabilities)		(313)
Total assets less current liabilities		6,687
Creditors: amounts falling due after more than one year		800
		5,887
Capital and reserves		
Called up share capital		1,000
Revaluation reserve		550
Profit and loss account		4,051
		5,601

Workings

1   *Fixed assets*

	Cost	Acc. Depn.	NBV
	£'000	£'000	£'000
Land	525		525
Buildings	1,000	50	950
Fixtures & fittings	1,170	117	1,053
Motor vehicles	1,520	380	1,140
Office equipment	350	70	280
	4,565	617	3,948

2   *Debtors*

	£'000	£'000
Trade debtors	857	
Plus accruals	104	
		961
Less prepayments		(37)
		924

3   *Creditors: amounts falling due within one year*

	£'000
Trade creditors	483
Corporation tax payable	382
Dividends payable	60
Provision for doubtful debts	61
10% Debentures	1,500
	2,486

4   *Creditors: amounts falling due after more than one year*

	£'000
Share premium	800

5   *Profit and loss account*

	£'000
At 1/4/X6	2,819
Retained profit for the year	1,232
At 31/3/X7	4,051

You have also received the following additional information to assist you in your task.

(a)   The share capital consists of ordinary shares with a nominal value of 25 pence. The company has paid an interim dividend during the year and the directors have recommended a final dividend of 6 pence per share, which has not been provided for in the extended trial balance.

(b)   The tax charge for the year has been estimated at £382,000.

(c)   The investments shown on the extended trial balance relate to long-term investment in the shares of one subsidiary undertaking and one associated company.

PRIMAVERA FASHIONS LTD
EXTENDED TRIAL BALANCE 31 MARCH 20X7

DESCRIPTION	TRIAL BALANCE Debit £'000	TRIAL BALANCE Credit £'000	ADJUSTMENTS Debit £'000	ADJUSTMENTS Credit £'000	PROFIT AND LOSS Debit £'000	PROFIT AND LOSS Credit £'000	BALANCE SHEET Debit £'000	BALANCE SHEET Credit £'000
Profit and loss account		2,819						2,819
Land - cost	525						525	
Buildings - cost	1,000						1,000	
Fixtures & fittings - cost	1,170						1,170	
Motor vehicles-cost	1,520						1,520	
Office equipment	350						350	
Sales		12,604				12,604		
Buildings-accumulated depreciation		170		50				220
Fixtures & fittings - accumulated depreciation		229		117				346
Motor vehicles - accumulated depreciation		203		380				583
Office equipment - accumulated depreciation		73		70				143
Stock	1,097		1,178	1,178	1,097	1,178	1,178	
Interest charges	153				153			
Goodwill	128						128	
Trade debtors	857						857	
Purchases	7,604				7,604			
Interim dividend	160				160			
Investments	2,924						2,924	
Cash at bank	152						152	
Distribution costs	1,444		68	17	1,495			
Administrative expenses	1,441		36	20	1,457			
Depreciation-buildings			50		50			
Depreciation-fixtures and fittings			117		117			
Depreciation-motor vehicles			380		380			
Depreciation-office equipment			70		70			
Share capital		1,000						1,000
Provision for doubtful debts		61						61
Trade creditors		483						483
Accruals				104				104
Dividends from subsidiary undertaking		23				23		
Prepayments			37				37	
Dividends from associated company		10				10		
10% Debentures		1,500						1,500
Share premium		800						800
Revaluation reserve		550						550
Profit					1,232			1,232
	20,525	20,525	1,936	1,936	13,815	13,815	9,841	9,841

Tasks

(a) Recraft the company balance sheet for Primavera Fashions Ltd as at 31 March 20X7. Make any changes that you feel to be necessary to the balance sheet and workings provided by the financial accountant using the information contained in the extended trial balance for the year ended 31 March 20X7.

Note. You are *not* required to produce a profit and loss account.

The directors of Primavera Fashions Ltd have asked you to prepare some answers to certain questions they have relating to the year end financial statements that are due to be considered at next week's meeting of the Board.

The directors are uncertain as to how the balance on the share premium account arose and how it can be used.

The directors have just learned that one of their trade debtors has gone into liquidation owing them £24,000. The liquidator has informed them that it is likely that there will be no assets available to pay off creditors and they wonder whether this will have any effect on the financial statements for the year ended 31 March 20X7. The directors are also uncertain as to the accounting treatment of their investment in shares of an associated company, Spring Ltd. Primavera Fashions Ltd purchased a 35% interest in the company for £400,000 in 20X5 when the total net assets of the company amounted to £800,000. (There was no goodwill shown in the associated company's own balance sheet.) Since acquisition Spring Ltd has made profits amounting to £200,000 and, as at 31 March 20X7, the total net assets of the company amounted to £1,000,000.

(b) Reply to the following questions from the directors. Where appropriate, justify your answers by reference to company law, accounting concepts and applicable accounting standards.

   (i)   (1) How did the balance on the share premium arise?

          (2) Can it be used to pay dividends to the shareholders?

          (3) Give one use of the share premium account.

   (ii) Will the fact that the debtor went into liquidation after the end of the financial year have any impact upon the financial statements for the year ended 31 March 20X7?

   (iii)   (1) At what amount will the investment in Spring Ltd be shown in the group balance sheet as at 31 March 20X7?

          (2) Show how the total investment in Spring Ltd will be analysed in the notes to the group financial statements.

(50 mins)

17 Solu

You have been asked to assist in the preparation of the financial statements of Solu Ltd for the year ended 31 March 20X8. The company runs a wholesale stationery and confectionery business for retailers. You have been provided with the extended trial balance of Solu Ltd for the year ended 31 March 20X8 which is set out on page 28.

You have also been given the following further information.

(a) The authorised and issued share capital of the business consists of ordinary shares with a nominal value of 25p.

SOLU LIMITED: EXTENDED TRIAL BALANCE 31 MARCH 20X8

Description	Trial balance Debit £'000	Trial balance Credit £'000	Adjustments Debit £'000	Adjustments Credit £'000	Profit and loss account Debit £'000	Profit and loss account Credit £'000	Balance sheet Debit £'000	Balance sheet Credit £'000
Land and buildings - cost	268						268	
Fixtures and fittings - cost	100						100	
Motor vehicles - cost	120						120	
Office equipment - cost	90						90	
Land and buildings - accumulated depreciation		50						50
Fixtures and fittings - accumulated depreciation		35						35
Motor vehicles - accumulated depreciation		65						65
Office equipment - accumulated depreciation		45						45
Investment in Edward	200						200	
Sales		4,090				4,090		
Purchases	1,800				1,800			
Stock	300		320	320	300	320	320	
Debtors	500						500	
Provision for bad debts		1						1
Prepayments			15				15	
Bank overdraft		55						55
Creditors		459						459
Accruals				40				40
Carriage inwards	25				25			
Distribution costs	1,050		10	5	1,055			
Administrative expenses	970		30	10	990			
Interest charges	10				10			
Interim dividend	32				32			
Share capital		400						400
Profit and loss account		65						65
Long-term loan		200						200
Profit					198			198
Total	5,465	5,465	375	375	4,410	4,410	1,613	1,613

(b)   The company has paid an interim dividend of 2p per share. The company wishes to allow a total dividend of 6p per share for the year.

(c)   The corporation tax charge for the year has been calculated as £75,000.

(d)   Depreciation has been charged on all assets for the year and included in the trial balance figures for distribution costs and administrative expenses.

(e)   The interest on the long-term loan is charged at 10% per annum. It is paid twice a year in arrears. The charge for the first six months of the year is included in the trial balance.

(f)   The general provision for bad debts is to be adjusted to 2% of debtors.

(g)   On 31 March 20X8 Solu Ltd bought 75% of the share capital of Edward Ltd for £200,000.

(h)   The share capital and reserves of Edward Ltd at that date were as follows.

	£
Ordinary share capital (£1)	100,000
Share premium account	50,000
Profit and loss account	25,000

The fixed assets of Edward Ltd were included in the balance sheet at a net book value of £70,000 but a valuation on 31 March 20X8 valued them at £95,000.

Tasks

(a)   Make the journal entries you feel to be necessary to the balances in the extended trial balance as a result of the matters set out in the further information above. Narratives are not required.

Notes

1   Ignore any effect of these adjustments on the tax charge for the year given above.

2   You must show any workings relevant to understanding your calculation of figures appearing in the financial statements.

(b)   Draft a profit and loss account for the year ended 31 March 20X8 (after adjustments made in task (a)).

Note. You are *not* required to prepare a statement of total recognised gains and losses or the reconciliation of movements in shareholders' funds required under FRS 3.

(c)   The directors have asked you a number of questions. Prepare notes to answer them referring to company law and accounting standards where appropriate.

(i)   An independent valuer has valued the land and buildings at £550,000. The directors have asked you if it is possible to show this valuation rather than the cost of the assets in the trial balance and, if so, to detail the entries needed to show the increased value of the fixed assets in the accounts.

(ii)   The directors understand that the accounts are prepared under the accruals concept. They are unsure what this means and have asked you to explain it briefly using one example from the accounts of Solu Ltd.

(iii)   The directors understand that Edward Ltd is now a subsidiary undertaking of Solu Ltd but they would like to have the definition of a subsidiary undertaking clarified. Define in simple terms a subsidiary undertaking according to FRS 2 *Accounting for subsidiary undertakings* and the Companies Act.

(d)   Calculate the minority interest in the Solu Group as at 31 March 20X8.

(80 mins)

18 Bathlea

You work as an assistant accountant in an accountancy firm. Your manager has asked you to help with the preparation of the financial statements of Bathlea Ltd for the year ended 30 September 20X8. The company operates a warehouse which distributes computer components. The bookkeeper has provided you with the extended trial balance of Bathlea Ltd for the year ended 30 September 20X8, which is set out on page 31.

The following further information has been supplied.

(a)   The authorised and issued share capital of the company consists of ordinary shares with a nominal value of £1.

(b)   The company has paid an interim dividend of 3p per share. The company wishes to provide for a final dividend of 5.5p per share.

(c)   The corporation tax charge for the year has been calculated as £11,000.

(d)   Depreciation has been charged on all assets for the year and included in the trial balance figures for distribution costs and administrative expenses.

(e)   The interest on the long-term loan is charged at 12% per annum and is paid monthly in arrears. The charge for the first eleven months of the year is included in the trial balance.

(f)   A debtor owing Bathlea Ltd £10,000 went into liquidation on 2 October 20X8. This has not been accounted for.

(g)   The general provision for bad debts is to be adjusted to 3% of debtors.

Tasks

(a)   Make the necessary journal entries as a result of the further information given above. Dates and narratives are not required.

Notes

1   Ignore any effect of these adjustments on the tax charge for the year given above.

2   You must show any workings relevant to these adjustments.

(b)   Draft a profit and loss account for the year ended 30 September 20X8 and a balance sheet as at that date (after adjustments made in task (a)).

(c)   The directors have asked you a number of questions. Prepare notes to answer them referring to accounting standards were appropriate.

(i)   There is a law suit pending against Bathlea Ltd. There is a remote possibility that it will result in Bathlea Ltd having to pay a customer compensation of £10,000 plus court costs. No account has been taken of this in the extended trial balance. The directors wish to know if it should be accrued.

BATHLEA LIMITED: EXTENDED TRIAL BALANCE 30 SEPTEMBER 20X8

Description	Trial balance Debit £'000	Trial balance Credit £'000	Adjustments Debit £'000	Adjustments Credit £'000	Profit and loss account Debit £'000	Profit and loss account Credit £'000	Balance sheet Debit £'000	Balance sheet Credit £'000
Land and buildings - cost	300						300	
Fixtures and fittings - cost	220						220	
Motor vehicles - cost	70						70	
Office equipment - cost	80						80	
Land and buildings - accumulated depreciation		65						65
Fixtures and fittings - accumulated depreciation		43						43
Motor vehicles - accumulated depreciation		27						27
Office equipment - accumulated depreciation		35						35
Sales		3,509				3,509		
Purchases	1,600				1,600			
Stock	200		250	250	200	250	250	
Debtors	370						370	
Provision for bad debts		5						5
Prepayments			10				10	
Bank overdraft		3						3
Creditors		350						350
Accruals				9				9
Carriage inwards	91				91			
Distribution costs	860		7	10	857			
Administrative expenses	890		2		892			
Interest charges	11				11			
Interim dividend	15				15			
Share capital		500						500
Profit and loss account		70						70
Long-term loan		100						100
Profit (loss)					93			93
Total	4,707	4,707	269	269	3,759	3,759	1,300	1,300

(ii) The directors are considering quite a large development project next year and would like to know the possible alternative accounting treatments for this expenditure in next year's accounts.

(60 mins)

19 Mattesich

The directors of Mattesich Ltd are to hold a board meeting next week to consider the performance of the company in the past year. They will also discuss the accounting policy for valuing fixed assets. The company accountant, who would normally prepare the documents for the meeting, is ill. He has completed the extended trial balance for the year ended 30 September 20X0 which is set out on page 33.

You have been given the following further information.

- The share capital of the business consists of ordinary shares with a nominal value of £1.

- The company paid an interim dividend of 15p per share this year and is proposing a final dividend of 20p per share.

- Depreciation has been calculated on all the fixed assets of the business and has already been entered into the distribution expenses and administrative expenses ledger balances as shown on the extended trial balance.

- The corporation tax charge for the year has been estimated at £3,813,000.

- Details of acquisitions and discontinued operations are as follows.

	Business acquired £'000	Discontinued operations £'000
Turnover	2,714	1,213
Cost of sales	950	788
Gross profit	1,764	425
Distribution costs	692	234
Administration expenses	469	178
Net profit	603	13

Task

Draft a profit and loss account for the year ended 30 September 20X0 using Format 1 in accordance with the Companies Act 1985 as supplemented by FRS 3 Reporting financial performance.

Notes

1 You do *not* need to prepare any of the notes to the financial statements that are required by FRS 3.

2 You do *not* need to prepare journal entries for any additional adjustments that may be necessary as a result of the further information given above.

3 You do *not* need to do an analysis of distribution costs and administrative expenses.

(40 mins)

MATTESICH LIMITED
EXTENDED TRIAL BALANCE 30 SEPTEMBER 20X0

DESCRIPTION	TRIAL BALANCE		ADJUSTMENTS		PROFIT AND LOSS		BALANCE SHEET	
	Debit £'000	Credit £'000	Debit £'000	Credit £'000	Debit £'000	Credit £'000	Debit £'000	Credit £'000
Buildings - accumulated depreciation		2,731						2,731
Office equipment - accumulated deprecation		2,456						2,456
Motor vehicles - accumulated depreciation		5,502						5,502
Fixtures and fittings - accumulated depreciation		2,698						2,698
Loss on disposal of discontinued operation	473				473			
Trade creditors		2,727						2,727
Debtors	6,654						6,654	
Distribution costs	5,695		206	38	5,863			
Administrative expenses	3,337		181	49	3,469			
Land - cost	8,721						8,721	
Buildings - cost	12,873						12,873	
Office equipment - cost	6,182						6,182	
Motor vehicles - cost	11,522						11,522	
Fixtures and fittings - cost	6,913						6,913	
Interest	544				544			
Sales		40,448				40,448		
Loan		6,800						6,800
Ordinary share capital		14,000						14,000
Stock	12,973		13,482	13,482	12,973	13,482	13,482	
Profit and loss account		12,214						12,214
Accruals				387				387
Share premium		7,200						7,200
Interim dividend	2,100				2,100			
Prepayments			87				87	
Cash in bank and in hand	107						107	
Purchases	18,682				18,682			
Profit					9,826			9,826
	96,776	96,776	13,956	13,956	53,930	53,930	66,541	66,541

BPP PROFESSIONAL EDUCATION

20 Brecked

You have been asked to help prepare the financial statements of Brecked plc for the year ended 31 March 20X1. The trial balance of the company as at 31 March 20X1 is set out below.

BRECKED PLC
TRIAL BALANCE AS AT 31 MARCH 20X1

	Debit £	Credit £
Trade creditors		2,307
Sales		21,383
Cash at bank	185	
Interest	400	
Trade debtors	3,564	
Land – cost	5,150	
Buildings – cost	3,073	
Fixtures and fittings – cost	2,169	
Motor vehicles – cost	4,609	
Office equipment – cost	927	
Interim dividend	450	
Ordinary share capital		3,000
Accruals		135
Long term loan		5,000
Distribution costs	2,017	
Administrative expenses	1,351	
Profit and loss account		5,340
Prepayments	92	
Share premium		1,500
Buildings – accumulated depreciation		420
Fixtures and fittings – accumulated depreciation		756
Motor vehicles – accumulated depreciation		2,014
Office equipment – accumulated depreciation		382
Stock as at 1 April 20X0	4,516	
Purchases	13,841	
Provision for doubtful debts		107
	42,344	42,344

Further information

(a) The authorised share capital of the company, all of which has been issued, consists of ordinary shares with a nominal value of £1.

(b) The company paid an interim dividend of 15p per share during the year but has not provided for the proposed final dividend of 10p per share.

(c) The stock at the close of business on 31 March 20X1 was valued at cost at £5,346,000.

(d) The corporation tax charge for the year has been calculated as £1,473,000.

(e)   Additions to fixed assets were:

Motor vehicles   £1,340,000
Office equipment   £268,000

Motor vehicles which had cost £975,000 and which had accumulated depreciation of £506,000 were disposed of during the year. There were no other additions or disposals. All of the additions and disposals have been included in the accounts as at 31 March 20X1.

(f)   No depreciation charges for the year have been entered into the accounts as at 31 March 20X1. The depreciation charges for the year are as follows.

	£'000
Buildings	65
Fixtures and fittings	217
Motor vehicles	648
Office equipment	185

(g)   The land has been revalued by professional valuers at £6,000,000. The revaluation is to be included in the financial statements for the year ended 31 March 20X1.

(h)   Legal proceedings have been started against Brecked Ltd because of faulty products supplied to a customer. The company's lawyers advise that it is probable that the entity will be found liable for damages of £250,000.

Tasks

(a)   Make the necessary journal entries as a result of the further information given above. Dates and narratives are not required.

Notes

(i)   You must show any workings relevant to these adjustments.
(ii)   Ignore any effect of these adjustments on the tax charge for the year given above.

(b)   Draft a note to the accounts showing movements on tangible fixed assets, as far as the information given allows.

(c)   Explain your treatment of the probable damages arising from the legal proceedings. Refer, where relevant, to accounting standards.

(50 mins)

21 Leger

You have been asked to help prepare the financial statements of Leger Ltd for the year ended 30 September 20X1 and to advise the directors on the regulatory framework for financial reporting. The trial balance of the company as at 30 September 20X1 is shown below.

LEGER LIMITED
TRIAL BALANCE AS AT 30 SEPTEMBER 20X1

	Debit £'000	Credit £'000
Trade creditors		1,042
Interest	180	
Trade debtors	3,665	
Stock as at 1 October 20X0	3,127	
Purchases	11,581	
Interim dividend	300	
Ordinary share capital		2,500
Accruals		92
9% debentures		4,000
Distribution costs	3,415	
Administrative expenses	2,607	
Land – cost	5,637	
Buildings – cost	3,615	
Fixtures and fittings – cost	2,871	
Motor vehicles – cost	1,526	
Office equipment – cost	1,651	
Profit and loss account		6,620
Revaluation reserve		1,000
Sales		21,324
Cash at bank	344	
Prepayments	84	
Share premium		1,000
Buildings – accumulated depreciation		1,147
Fixtures and fittings – accumulated depreciation		963
Motor vehicles – accumulated depreciation		784
Office equipment – accumulated depreciation		214
Carriage inwards	83	
	40,686	40,686

Further information

(a) The authorised share capital of the company, all of which has been issued, consists of ordinary shares with a nominal value of £1.

(b) The company paid an interim dividend of 12p per share during the year but has not provided for the proposed final dividend of 15p per share.

(c) The stock at the close of business on 30 September 20X1 was valued at cost at £5,408,000.

(d) The corporation tax charge for the year has been calculated as £1,567,000.

(e) Interest on the debentures has not been paid or charged in the accounts for the last six months of the year.

(f) Land and buildings were revalued during the year. The depreciation charge of £72,000 relating to the buildings has been calculated on the revalued amount and entered in the accounts in the trial balance. The depreciation charge calculated on the original historical cost of the buildings would have been £62,000.

(g) All of the operations of the business are continuing operations. There were no acquisitions in the year.

Tasks

(a) Draft a profit and loss account for the year ended 30 September 20X1
(b) Prepare a note on historical cost profits and losses as required by FRS 3.

(35 mins)

22 Typeset

You have been assigned to assist in the preparation of the financial statements of Typeset Ltd for the year ended 31 March 20X9. The company is a wholesale distributor of desktop publishing equipment. You have been provided with the extended trial balance of Typeset Ltd as at 31 March 20X9 which is set out on page 38.

You have been given the following further information.

(a) The authorised share capital of the business, all of which has been issued, consists of ordinary shares with a nominal value of £1.

(b) Depreciation has been calculated on a monthly basis on all of the fixed assets of the business and has already been entered into the distribution costs and administration expenses ledger balances as shown on the extended trial balance.

(c) The corporation tax charge for the year has been calculated as £493,000.

(d) The company has paid an interim dividend of 5p per share during the year but has not provided for the proposed final dividend of 7p per share.

(e) One of the customers who owed the company £36,000 at the end of the year is in financial difficulties. The directors have estimated that only half of this amount is likely to be paid. No adjustment has been made for this in the extended trial balance. The general provision for doubtful debts is to be maintained at 2% of the remaining debtors excluding the £36,000 balance.

Task

Making any adjustments required as a result of the further information provided, draft a balance sheet for Typeset Ltd as at 31 March 20X9.

Notes

1 You are not required to produce notes to the accounts.

2 You must show any workings relevant to understanding your calculation of figures appearing in the financial statements.

3 You are not required to produce journal entries for any adjustments to the figures in the extended trial balance that are required.

4 You should ignore any effect of these adjustments on the tax charge for the year as given above.

(30 mins)

TYPSET LIMITED
EXTENDED TRIAL BALANCE 31 MARCH 20X9

Description	Trial balance		Adjustments		Profit and loss account		Balance sheet	
	Debit	Credit	Debit	Credit	Debit	Credit	Debit	Credit
	£'000	£'000	£'000	£'000	£'000	£'000	£'000	£'000
Trade debtors	3,136						3,136	
Cash at bank	216						216	
Interest	125				125			
Profit and loss account		3,533						3,533
Provision for doubtful debts		37						37
Distribution costs	3,549		59	36	3,572			
Administrative expenses	3,061		63	61	3,063			
Revaluation reserve		500						500
Sales		18,757				18,757		
Land – cost	2,075						2,075	
Buildings – cost	2,077						2,077	
Fixtures and fittings – cost	1,058						1,058	
Motor vehicles – cost	2,344						2,344	
Office equipment – cost	533						533	
Stock	3,921		4,187	4,187	3,921	4,187	4,187	
Purchases	10,582				10,582			
Interim dividend	250				250			
Trade creditors		1,763						1,763
Buildings – accumulated depreciation		383						383
Fixtures and fittings – accumulated depreciation		495						495
Motor vehicles – accumulated depreciation		1,237						1,237
Office equipment – accumulated depreciation		152						152
Prepayments			97				97	
Ordinary share capital		5,000						5,000
Share premium		1,200						1,200
Accruals				122				122
Investments	1,580						1,580	
Long-term loan		1,450						1,450
Profit					1,431			1,431
TOTAL	34,507	34,507	4,406	4,406	22,944	22,944	17,303	17,303

chapter 10

Cash flow statements

Activity checklist

This checklist shows which performance criteria, range statement or knowledge and understanding point is covered by each activity in this chapter. Tick off each activity as you complete it.

Activity

23		Range Statement for 11.1: cash flow statement
24		Range Statement for 11.1: cash flow statement
25		Performance Criteria 11.1.D: prepare and interpret a limited company cash flow statement
26		Performance Criteria 11.1.D: prepare and interpret a limited company cash flow statement
27		Performance Criteria 11.1.D: prepare and interpret a limited company cash flow statement

23 Paton

You have been asked to assist in the preparation of financial statements for Paton Ltd for the year ended 30 September 20X1. The profit and loss account and balance sheets of Paton Ltd are set out below.

PATON LIMITED
PROFIT AND LOSS ACCOUNT FOR THE YEAR 30 SEPTEMBER 20X1

	£'000
Turnover	24,732
Cost of sales	11,129
Gross profit	13,603
Profit on the sale of fixed assets	131
Distribution costs	4,921
Administration expenses	2,875
Profit on ordinary activities before interest	5,938
Interest paid and similar charges	392
Profit on ordinary activities before taxation	5,546
Tax on profit on ordinary activities	1,821
Profit for the financial year	3,725
Dividends	1,500
Retained profit for the financial year	2,225

PATON LIMITED
BALANCE SHEET AS AT 30 SEPTEMBER 20X1

	20X1		20X0	
	£'000	£'000	£'000	£'000
Fixed assets		13,383		9,923
Investment in MacNeal Ltd		5,000		
Current assets				
Stock assets	7,420		6,823	
Trade debtors	4,122		3,902	
Cash	102		1,037	
	11,644		11,762	
Current liabilities				
Trade creditors	1,855		1,432	
Dividends payable	900		700	
Taxation	1,821		1,327	
	4,576		3,459	
		7,068		8,303
Long term loan		(5,000)		(1,500)
		20,451		16,726
Capital and reserves				
Called up share capital		10,000		9,000
Share premium		3,500		3,000
Profit and loss account		6,951		4,726
		20,451		16,726

You have been given the following further information.

- A fixed asset costing £895,000 with accumulated depreciation of £372,000 was sold in the year. The total depreciation charge for the year was £2,007,000.
- All sales and purchases were on credit. Other expenses were paid for in cash.

Task

Provide a reconciliation of operating profit to net cash flows from operating activities for Paton Ltd for the year ended 30 September 20X1.

(15 mins)

24 Fun and games

The directors of Fun Ltd have a number of questions relating to the financial statements of their recently acquired subsidiary undertaking, Games Ltd. Fun Ltd acquired 75% of the ordinary share capital of Games Ltd on 30 September 20X8 for £2,244,000. The fair value of the fixed assets in Games Ltd as at 30 September 20X8 was £2,045,000. The directors have provided you with the balance sheet of Games Ltd as at 30 September 20X8 along with some further information.

GAMES LIMITED
BALANCE SHEET AS AT 30 SEPTEMBER 20X8

	20X8	20X7
	£'000	£'000
Fixed assets	1,845	1,615
Current assets		
Stocks	918	873
Trade debtors	751	607
Cash	23	87
	1,692	1,567
Current liabilities		
Trade creditors	583	512
Dividends payable	52	48
Taxation	62	54
	697	614
Net current assets	995	953
Long term loan	560	420
	2,280	2,148
Capital and reserves		
Called up share capital	1,000	1,000
Share premium	100	100
Profit and loss account	1,180	1,048
	2,280	2,148

Further information

(a) No fixed assets were sold during the year. The depreciation charge for the year amounted to £277,000.

(b) All sales and purchases were on credit. Other expenses were paid for in cash.

(c) The profit on ordinary activities before taxation was £246,000. Interest of £56,000 was charged in the year.

41

Tasks

(a) Provide a reconciliation between cash flows from operating activities and operating profit for Games Ltd for the year ended 30 September 20X8.

You are *not* required to prepare a cash flow statement.

(b) Prepare notes to take to the Board meeting to answer the following questions of the directors.

(i) What figure for the minority interest would appear in the consolidated balance sheet of Fun Ltd as at 30 September 20X8?

(ii) Where in the balance sheet would the minority interest be disclosed?

(iii) What is a 'minority interest'?

(40 mins)

25 Edlin

You have been given the financial statements of Edlin Ltd for the year ended 31 March 20X8, with comparative figures for the year ended 31 March 20X7. The company is expanding and is in the middle of a major programme of replacing all of its fixed assets.

EDLIN LIMITED
PROFIT AND LOSS ACCOUNT FOR THE YEAR ENDED 31 MARCH

	20X8		20X7	
	£'000	£'000	£'000	£'000
Turnover, continuing operations		3,000		2,000
Cost of sales: opening stock	200		150	
purchases	1,700		1,250	
closing stock	(220)		(200)	
		1,680		1,200
Gross profit		1,320		800
Depreciation		175		150
Other expenses		500		400
Profit on sale of fixed asset		5		-
Operating profit for the year		650		250
Interest paid		15		12
Profit before tax		635		238
Taxation on profit		100		35
Profit after tax		535		203
Proposed dividends		100		50
Retained profit		435		153
Retained profit (loss) b/f		115		(38)
Retained profit c/f		550		115

EDLIN LIMITED
BALANCE SHEET AS AT 31 MARCH

	20X8		20X7	
	£'000	£'000	£'000	£'000
Fixed assets		552		200
Stock	220		200	
Debtors	250		160	
Cash	218		20	
	688		380	
Current liabilities				
Trade creditors	150		110	
Dividends payable	100		50	
Taxation	100		35	
	350		195	
Net current assets		338		185
Total assets less current liabilities		890		385
Long term liabilities				
Long-term loan		150		120
		740		265
Capital and reserves				
Called up share capital		120		100
Share premium account		70		50
Profit and loss account		550		115
		740		265

The following further information is provided.

(a)   In July 20X7 an asset was sold which had originally cost £20,000 and was purchased by the company in July 20X4. Fixed assets are depreciated on a straight line basis at 20%. The policy is to charge a full year's depreciation in the year of purchase and none in the year of sale.

(b)   A new asset was purchased for £535,000 during the year.

(c)   Sales and purchases were on credit with all other expenses (including interest) being paid in cash.

(d)   There was a share issue during the year.

Tasks

(a)   Prepare a reconciliation between cash flows from operating activities and operating profit for the year ended 31 March 20X8.

(b)   Prepare a cash flow statement for the year ended 31 March 20X8 in accordance with FRS 1 (revised).

(c)   Calculate the gearing and current ratios for Edlin for 20X8 and 20X7 and briefly comment on the ratios.

(30 mins)

43

26 Angle

You have been asked to assist in the preparation of financial statements for Angle Ltd for the year ended 31 March 20X1. The profit and loss account and balance sheets of the company are set out below.

ANGLE LIMITED
PROFIT AND LOSS ACCOUNT FOR THE YEAR ENDED 31 MARCH 20X1

	20X1 £'000
Turnover	
Continuing operations	8,975
Cost of sales	5,013
Gross profit	3,962
Distribution costs	1,172
Administration expenses	953
Operating profit	
Continuing operations	1,837
Interest paid and similar charges	202
Profit on ordinary activities before taxation	1,635
Tax on profit on ordinary activities	490
Profit for the financial year	1,145
Dividends	450
Retained profit for the financial year	695

ANGLE LIMITED
BALANCE SHEET AS AT 31 MARCH 20X1

	20X1		20X0	
	£'000	£'000	£'000	£'000
Fixed assets		7,287		4,009
Current assets				
Stocks	1,982		1,346	
Trade debtors	812		1,086	
Cash	433		82	
	3,227		2,514	
Current liabilities				
Trade creditors	423		397	
Dividends payable	450		400	
Taxation	490		370	
	1,363		1,167	
Net current assets		1,864		1,347
Long term loan		(2,500)		(1,500)
		6,651		3,856
Capital and reserves				
Called up share capital		3,000		2,200
Share premium		1,200		400
Revaluation reserve		500		-
Profit and loss account		1,951		1,256
		6,651		3,856

Further information

(a) Land included in the fixed assets was valued at market value at the end of the year by a professional valuer at £500,000 greater than book value. The valuation has been incorporated into the financial statements of the company as at 31 March 20X1.

(b) No fixed assets were sold during the year to 31 March 20X1. Depreciation has been calculated on the fixed assets of the business and has already been entered in the profit and loss account. The charge for the year was £875,000.

(c) All sales and purchases were on credit. Other expenses were paid for in cash.

(d) Net cash inflow from operating activities for the year was £2,376,000. There was no over/underprovision of corporation tax for 20X0.

Task

Prepare a cash flow statement for Angle Ltd for the year ended 31 March 20X1 in accordance with the requirements of FRS 1 (revised).

Note. You are not required to provide a reconciliation between cash flows from operating activities and operating profit, or to produce any of the notes required by FRS 1.

(25 mins)

45

27 Roth

You have been asked to comment on the decline in the cash balance of Roth Co Ltd in 20X1. The cash flow statement of Roth Co Ltd is set out below to assist you in your analysis.

ROTH CO LIMITED
CASH FLOW STATEMENT
FOR THE YEAR ENDED 30 SEPTEMBER 20X1

	£'000	£'000
Net cash inflow from operating activities		5,959
Returns on investments and servicing of finance		
Interest paid		(542)
Taxation		(2,017)
Capital expenditure		
Payments to acquire tangible fixed assets	(1,432)	
Receipts from sale of tangible fixed assets	373	
		(1,059)
Equity dividends paid		(5,000)
		(2,659)
Financing		
Loan		1,050
Decrease in cash		(1,609)

ROTH CO LIMITED
RECONCILIATION OF OPERATING PROFIT
TO NET CASH INFLOW FROM OPERATING ACTIVITIES

	£'000
Operating profit	8,763
Depreciation charges	1,847
Increase in stock	(36)
Increase in debtors	(3,584)
Decrease in creditors	(1,031)
Net cash inflow from operating activities	5,959

Further information

- Sales and purchases for the company were similar in each of the two years.
- The cash balance at 30 September 20X1 was £234,000.

Task

Using the cash flow statement and the further information provided, prepare notes to explain why the cash balance has fallen in 20X1.

(20 mins)

chapter 11

Ratio analysis

Activity checklist

This checklist shows which performance criteria, range statement or knowledge and understanding point is covered by each activity in this chapter. Tick off each activity as you complete it.

Activity

28		Performance Criteria 11.2.D to 11.2.F
29		Performance Criteria 11.2.D to 11.2.F
30		Performance Criteria 11.2.D to 11.2.F
31		Performance Criteria 11.2.D to 11.2.F
32		Performance Criteria 11.2.D to 11.2.F

28 Magnus Carter

Magnus Carter has recently inherited a majority shareholding in a company, Baron Ltd. The company supplies camping equipment to retail outlets. Magnus wishes to be involved in the management of the business, but until now he has only worked in not-for-profit organisations. He would like to understand how the company has performed over the past two years and how efficient it is in using its recources. He has asked you to help him to interpret the financial statements of the company which are set out below.

BARON LIMITED
SUMMARY PROFIT AND LOSS ACCOUNTS
FOR THE YEAR ENDED 31 MARCH

	20X1	20X0
	£'000	£'000
Turnover	1,852	1,691
Cost of sales	648	575
Gross profit	1,204	1,116
Expenses	685	524
Profit before tax	519	592
Tax	125	147
Profit after tax	394	445
Dividends	250	325
Retained profit	144	120

BARON LIMITED
SUMMARY BALANCE SHEETS AS AT 31 MARCH

	20X1		20X0	
	£'000	£'000	£'000	£'000
Fixed assets		1,431		1,393
Current assets				
Stocks	217		159	
Debtors	319		236	
Cash	36		147	
	572		542	
Current liabilities				
Trade creditors	48		44	
Proposed dividend	250		325	
Taxation	125		130	
	423		499	
Net current assets		149		43
		1,580		1,436
Share capital		500		500
Profit and loss account		1,080		936
		1,580		1,436

Task

Prepare a report for Magnus Carter that includes:

(a)   A calculation of the following ratios for the two years:

      (i)   Gross profit percentage

      (ii)   Net profit percentage

      (iii)   Debtor turnover in days (debtor payment period)

      (iv)   Creditor turnover in days (creditor payment period based on cost of sales)

      (v)   Stock turnover in days (stock turnover period based on cost of sales)

(b)   For each ratio calculate:

(i)   A brief explanation in general terms of the meaning of the ratio

(ii)   Comments on how the performance or efficiency in the use of resources has changed over the two years

(c)   A statement, with reasons, identifying the areas that could be improved over the next year as indicated by the ratios and analysis performed.

(40 mins)

29 Bins

You have been asked by the directors of Bins Ltd, a distributor of domestic and industrial refuse containers, to analyse the financial statements of a potential supplier. They have identified a company called Gone Ltd as a potential supplier of containers. They have obtained the latest financial statements of the company, in summary form, which are set out below:

GONE LIMITED
SUMMARY PROFIT AND LOSS ACCOUNTS
FOR THE YEAR ENDED 31 DECEMBER

	20X7	20X6
	£'000	£'000
Turnover	1,800	1,300
Cost of sales	1,098	715
Gross profit	702	585
Expenses	504	315
Net profit before interest and tax	198	270

GONE LIMITED
SUMMARY BALANCE SHEETS
AS AT 31 DECEMBER

	20X7		20X6	
	£'000	£'000	£'000	£'000
Fixed assets		3,463		1,991
Current assets	460		853	
Current liabilities	(383)		(406)	
Net current assets		77		447
Long-term loan		(1,506)		(500)
		2,034		1,938
Share capital		800		800
Revaluation reserve		164		164
Profit and loss account		1,070		974
		2,034		1,938

The industry average ratios are as follows.

	20X7	20X6
Return on capital employed	13.4%	13.0%
Gross profit percentage	44.5%	43.2%
Net profit percentage	23.6%	23.2%
Current ratio	2.0:1	1.9:1
Gearing	36%	34%

Task

Prepare a report for the directors recommending whether or not to use Gone Ltd as a supplier for Bins Ltd given the information contained in the financial statements and the industry averages supplied. Your answer should comment on the profitability, liquidity and the level of gearing in the company, and how they have changed over the two years, and compare it with the industry as a whole. The report should include calculation of the following ratios for the two years.

(a) Return on capital employed
(b) Gross profit percentage
(c) Net profit percentage
(d) Current ratio
(e) Gearing

(35 mins)

30 Byrne and May

Duncan Tweedy wishes to invest some money in one of two private companies. He has obtained the latest financial statements for Byrne Ltd and May Ltd prepared for internal purposes. As part of his decision making process he has asked you to assess the relative profitability of the two companies. The financial statements of the companies are set out below.

SUMMARY PROFIT AND LOSS ACCOUNT
FOR THE YEAR ENDED 30 SEPTEMBER 20X0

	Byrne Limited £'000	May Limited £'000
Turnover	5,761	2,927
Cost of sales	2,362	966
Gross profit	3,399	1,961
Distribution costs	922	468
Administrative expenses	1,037	439
Operating profit	1,440	1,054
Interest paid and similar charges	152	40
Profit on ordinary activities before taxation	1,288	1,014
Tax on profit on ordinary activities	309	243
Profit for the financial year	979	771
Dividends	312	141
Retained profit for the financial year	667	630

SUMMARY BALANCE SHEET
FOR THE YEAR ENDED 30 SEPTEMBER 20X0

	Byrne Limited		May Limited	
	£'000	£'000	£'000	£'000
Fixed assets		6,188		2,725
Current assets	1,522		1,102	
Current liabilities	1,015		545	
Net current assets		507		557
Long term loan		(1,900)		(500)
		4,795		2,782
Capital and reserves				
Called up share capital: ordinary shares of £1 each		2,083		939
Profit and loss account		2,712		1,843
		4,795		2,782

You have also been given the following ratios.

	Byrne Limited	May Limited
Return on capital employed	21.5%	32.1%
Gross profit percentage	59.0%	67.0%
Net profit percentage	25.0%	36.0%
Earnings per share	47p	82p

Task

Prepare a report for Duncan Tweedy that:

(a)   Explains the meaning of each ratio
(b)   Uses each ratio to comment on the relative profitability of the companies
(c)   Concludes, with reasons, which company is the more profitable

(30 mins)

31 Animalets

Animalets plc is a large company with a number of subsidiaries. The group manufactures and distributes pet food and pet accessories. It is considering buying some shares in Superpet Ltd, a small company which makes toys and novelties for pets.

You have been given the financial statements for Superpet Ltd for the year ended 30 September 20X8.

SUPERPET LIMITED
PROFIT AND LOSS ACCOUNT FOR THE YEAR ENDED 30 SEPTEMBER 20X8

		20X8		20X7
	£'000	£'000	£'000	£'000
Turnover, continuing operations		2,000		1,500
Cost of sales: opening stock	300		200	
purchases	900		800	
closing stock	(350)		(300)	
		850		700
Gross profit		1,150		800
Depreciation		65		50
Other expenses		132		118
Profit on sale of fixed asset		5		-
Operating profit for the year		958		632
Interest paid		10		7
Profit before tax		948		625
Taxation on profit		300		200
Profit after tax		648		425
Proposed dividends		180		100
Retained profit		468		325
Retained profit b/f		450		125
Retained profit c/f		918		450

SUPERPET LIMITED
BALANCE SHEET AS AT 30 SEPTEMBER 20X8

	20X8		20X9	
	£'000	£'000	£'000	£'000
Fixed assets		1,138		638
Current assets				
Stock	350		300	
Debtors	400		250	
Cash	120		60	
	870		610	
Current liabilities				
Trade creditors	190		148	
Dividends payable	180		100	
Taxation	300		200	
	670		448	
Net current assets		200		162
Total assets less current liabilities		1,338		800
Long term liabilities				
Long term loan		(100)		(70)
		1,238		730
Capital and reserves				
Called up share capital		220		200
Share premium account		50		30
Revaluation reserve		50		50
Profit and loss account		918		450
		1,238		730

Tasks

(a)   Prepare a report to the directors of Animalets plc which considers Superpet's position and performance. Your report should be based on the following ratios only.

(i)   Gross profit ratio
(ii)   Current ratio
(iii)   Acid test (quick) ratio
(iv)   Gearing ratio

You are not expected to include recommendations in your report.

(b)   The directors of Animalets want to know how much cash Superpet received from operating activities for the year ended 30 September 20X8. Prepare a reconciliation of operating profit to cash flow from operating activities for this period.

(35 mins)

32 Gint

Georgina Grieg is deciding whether to lend some money to Gint Ltd. She has asked you to comment on the financial position of the company and to explain certain aspects of the financial statements of the company. She has given you the financial statements of Gint Ltd.

GINT LIMITED
PROFIT AND LOSS ACCOUNTS
FOR THE YEAR ENDED 31 MARCH

	20X1	20X0
	£'000	£'000
Turnover	3,851	3,413
Cost of sales	2,002	1,775
Gross profit	1,849	1,638
Distribution costs	782	737
Administrative expenses	515	491
Operating profit	552	410
Interest paid and similar charges	46	41
Profit on ordinary activities before taxation	506	369
Tax on profit on ordinary activities	126	92
Profit for the financial year	380	277
Dividends	160	140
Retained profit for the financial year	220	137

GINT LIMITED
BALANCE SHEETS AS AT 31 MARCH

	20X1		20X0	
	£'000	£'000	£'000	£'000
Fixed assets		4,372		4,341
Current assets				
Stocks	1,157		716	
Debtors	446		509	
Prepayments	23		19	
Cash at bank	37		57	
	1,663		1,301	
Current liabilities				
Trade creditors	406		392	
Accruals	31		26	
Dividends payable	160		140	
Taxation	126		92	
	723		650	
Net current assets		940		651
Long term loan		(600)		(500)
		4,712		4,492
Capital and reserves				
Called up share capital: ordinary shares of £1 each		1,000		1,000
Profit and loss account		3,712		3,492
		4,712		4,492

Tasks

Write a letter to Georgina Grieg that includes the following.

(a)   A calculation of the following ratios of Gint Ltd for each of the two years.

   (i)   Current ratio
   (i)   Quick ratio/acid test
   (iii)   Gearing ratio
   (iv)   Interest cover

(b)   An explanation of the meaning of each ratio

(c)   Comments on the financial position of Gint Ltd as shown by the ratios

(d)   A statement on how the financial position has changed over the two years covered by the financial statements

(e)   A conclusion on whether Georgina Grieg should lend money to Gint Ltd. Base your conclusion only on the ratios calculated and analysis performed

(35 mins)

chapter 12

Introduction to group accounts

Activity checklist

This checklist shows which performance criteria, range statement or knowledge and understanding point is covered by each activity in this chapter. Tick off each activity as you complete it.

Activity

| 33 | | Knowledge & Understanding point: general principles of consolidation |
| 34 | | Knowledge & Understanding point: general principles of consolidation |

33 Two options

The directors of Animalets are considering the following two options.

(a)   The purchase of 30% of the share capital in Superpet, which would give the directors of Animalets significant influence over Superpet

or

(b)   The purchase of 75% of the share capital in Superpet, which would give the directors of Animalets dominant influence over Superpet

Either option would constitute a participating interest in Superpet.

Explain briefly how these two different options would be accounted for in the consolidated profit and loss account and balance sheet of the Animalets Group.

(15 mins)

34 MacNeal

Paton Ltd has one subsidiary undertaking, MacNeal Ltd, which it acquired on 30 September 20X0. The balance sheet of MacNeal Ltd as at 30 September is set out below.

MACNEAL LIMITED
BALANCE SHEET AS AT 30 SEPTEMBER 20X0

	£'000	£'000
Fixed assets		4,844
Current assets	3,562	
Current liabilities	1,706	
Net current assets		1,856
Long term loan		(1,900)
		4,800
Capital and reserves		
Called up share capital		1,200
Share premium		800
Profit and loss account		2,800
		4,800

You have been given the following further information.

(a)   The share capital of MacNeal Ltd consists of ordinary shares of £1 each.

(b)   Paton Ltd acquired 900,000 shares in MacNeal Ltd on 30 September 20X0 at a cost of £5,000,000.

(c)   The fair value of the fixed assets of MacNeal Ltd at 30 September 20X0 was £5,844,000. The revaluation has not been reflected in the books of MacNeal Ltd.

Task

Calculate the goodwill on consolidation that arose on the acquisition of MacNeal Ltd on 30 September 20X0.

(15 mins)

chapters 13 and 14

Further aspects
of group accounting

35 Norman

You have been asked to assist in the preparation of the consolidated accounts of the Norman Group. Set out below are the balance sheets of Norman Ltd and Saxon Ltd for the year ended 31 March 20X1.

BALANCE SHEETS AS AT 31 MARCH 20X1

	Norman Limited		Saxon Limited	
	£'000	£'000	£'000	£'000
Tangible fixed assets		12,995		1,755
Investment in Saxon Ltd		1,978		–
Current assets				
Stocks	3,586		512	
Debtors	2,193		382	
Cash	84		104	
	5,863		998	
Current liabilities				
Trade creditors	1,920		273	
Proposed dividend	160		–	
Taxation	667		196	
	2,747		469	
Net current assets		3,116		529
Long term loan		–		(400)
		18,089		1,884
Share capital and reserves				
Share capital		2,000		1,000
Share premium		–		200
Profit and loss account		16,089		684
		18,089		1,884

Further information

(a) The share capital of both Norman Ltd and Saxon Ltd consists of ordinary shares of £1 each. There have been no changes to the balances of share capital and share premium during the year. No dividends were paid by Saxon Ltd during the year.

(b) Norman Ltd acquired 750,000 shares in Saxon Ltd on 31 March 20X0.

(c) At 31 March 20X0 the balance on the profit and loss account of Saxon Ltd was £424,000.

(d) The fair value of the fixed assets of Saxon Ltd at 31 March 20X0 was £2,047,000 as compared with their book value of £1,647,000. The revaluation has not been reflected in the books of Saxon Ltd. (Ignore any depreciation implications.)

(e) Goodwill arising on consolidation is to be amortised using the straight-line method over a period of 10 years.

Task

Prepare the consolidated balance sheet of Norman Ltd and its subsidiary undertaking as at 31 March 20X1.

(40 mins)

36 Checkoff

The finance director of Checkoff plc has asked you to prepare the draft consolidated profit and loss account for the group. The company has one subsidiary undertaking, Pooshkin Ltd. The profit and loss accounts of the two companies, prepared for internal purposes, for the year ended 31 March 20X1 are set out below.

PROFIT AND LOSS ACCOUNTS
FOR THE YEAR ENDED 31 MARCH 20X1

	Checkoff plc	Pooshkin Ltd
	£'000	£'000
Turnover	15,800	5,400
Cost of sales	8,500	2,800
Gross profit	7,300	2,600
Distribution costs	1,800	650
Administrative expenses	1,500	580
Dividends received from Pooshkin Ltd	300	–
Profit on ordinary activities before interest	4,300	1,370
Interest paid and similar charges	800	120
Profit on ordinary activities before taxation	3,500	1,250
Tax on profit on ordinary activities	1,120	370
Profit on ordinary activities after taxation	2,380	880
Dividends	750	400
Retained profit for the financial year	1,630	480

Further information

(a) Checkoff plc acquired 75% of the ordinary share capital of Pooshkin Ltd on 1 April 20X0.

(b) During the year Pooshkin Ltd sold stock which had cost £600,000, to Checkoff plc for £1,000,000. All of the stock had been sold by Checkoff plc by the end of the year.

(c) Ignore any write-off of goodwill for the period.

Task

Draft a consolidated profit and loss account for the Checkoff plc and its subsidiary undertaking for the year ended 31 March 20X1.

(25 mins)

Full Exam based Assessments

JUNE 2002 EXAM PAPER

TECHNICIAN STAGE – NVQ4

Unit 11

Drafting Financial Statements
(Accounting Practice, Industry and Commerce)

Time allowed – 3 hours plus 15 minutes' reading time

Answer **all** questions.

BPP note

This exam has been amended to reflect the form and content of the new standards.

DO NOT OPEN THIS PAPER UNTIL YOU ARE READY TO START
UNDER EXAM CONDITIONS

COVERAGE OF PERFORMANCE CRITERIA

All Unit 11 performance criteria are covered in this exam.

INSTRUCTIONS

This examination paper is in TWO sections.

You have to show competence in BOTH sections.

You should therefore attempt and aim to complete EVERY task in BOTH sections.

You should spend about 125 minutes on Section 1 and 55 minutes on Section 2.

You are allowed **three hours** to complete your work.

Write your answers in the answer booklet provided. If you require additional answer pages, ask the person in charge.

You may pull apart and rearrange your booklets if you wish to do so, but you must put them back in their original order before handing them in.

Correcting fluid may be used but should be used in moderation. Errors should be crossed out neatly and clearly. You should write in blue or black ink, not pencil.

A high level of accuracy is required. Check your work carefully before handing it in.

A full answer to this exam is given on page 153 of this Kit.

Section 1

You should spend about 125 minutes on this Section. This Section is in three parts.

Part A

You should spend about 45 minutes on this part.

Data

Lawton Ltd paid £500,000 to acquire 300,000 ordinary shares in Doig Ltd on 1 May 20X0 when the profit and loss account of Doig Ltd was £140,000. The following are the summarised financial statements of the two companies for the financial year ended 30 April 20X3

PROFIT AND LOSS ACCOUNTS FOR THE YEAR ENDED 30 APRIL 20X3

	Lawton Limited	Doig Limited
	£'000	£'000
Turnover	3,400	1,200
Cost of sales	2,300	820
Gross profit	1,100	380
Distribution costs	260	80
Administrative expenses	200	60
Operating profit	640	240
Investment income	64	0
Profit on ordinary activities before taxation	704	240
Taxation on profit on ordinary activities	200	60
Profit on ordinary activities after taxation	504	180
Proposed ordinary dividends	280	80
Retained profit for the year	224	100

BALANCE SHEETS AS AT 30 APRIL 20X3

	Lawton Limited £'000	Lawton Limited £'000	Doig Limited £'000	Doig Limited £'000
Fixed assets				
Total assets at net book value		1,300		360
Investment				
Shares in Doig Ltd at cost		500		
Current assets				
Stock, at cost	660		220	
Debtors	540		280	
Bank	240		140	
	1,440		640	
Creditors: amounts falling due within one year				
Creditors	180		140	
Proposed dividends	280		80	
Corporation tax	220		60	
	680		280	
Net current assets		760		360
		2,560		720
Capital and reserves				
£1 Ordinary shares		1,800		400
Profit and loss account		760		320
		2,560		720

The following information is also available.

(a) During the year Lawton Ltd sold goods which originally cost £300,000 to Doig Ltd. Lawton Ltd invoiced Doig Ltd at cost plus 20%. These goods had all been sold by Doig Ltd by 30 April 20X3.

(b) Doig Ltd's creditors includes £40,000 owing to Lawton Ltd.

(c) Lawton Ltd has recognised the dividends proposed by Doig Ltd in its profit and loss account.

(d) Lawton Ltd's policy is to amortise goodwill equally over five years. The goodwill on acquisition of Doig Ltd was £95,000.

TASK 1.1

Prepare the following for Lawton Ltd.

(a) The consolidated profit and loss account for the year ended 30 April 20X3
(b) The consolidated balance sheet as at 30 April 20X3

Disclosure notes are not required.

Part B

You should spend about 50 minutes on this part.

You have been asked to help prepare the financial statements of Kentish Ltd for the year ended 31 December 20X3 and to advise the directors on the regulatory framework for financial reporting. The trial balance of the company as at 31 December 20X3 is shown below.

KENTISH LIMITED
TRIAL BALANCE AS AT 31 DECEMBER 20X3

	Debit £'000	Credit £'000
9% debentures		12,000
Accruals		276
Administrative expenses	7,821	
Buildings – cost	10,845	
Buildings – accumulated depreciation		3,441
Carriage inwards	249	
Cash at bank	1,032	
Distribution costs	10,245	
Fixtures and fittings – cost	8,613	
Fixtures and fittings – accumulated depreciation		2,889
Interest	540	
Interim dividend	900	
Land – cost	16,911	
Motor vehicles – cost	4,578	
Motor vehicles – accumulated depreciation		2,352
Office equipment – cost	4,953	
Office equipment – accumulated depreciation		642
Ordinary share capital		7,500
Prepayments	252	
Profit and loss account		19,860
Purchases	34,743	
Revaluation reserve		3,000
Sales		63,972
Share premium		3,000
Stock as at 1 January 20X3	9,381	
Trade creditors		3,126
Trade debtors	10,995	
	122,058	122,058

Further information

(a) The authorised share capital of the company, all of which has been issued, consists of ordinary shares with a nominal value of £1.

(b) The company paid an interim dividend of 12p per share during the year but has not provided for the proposed final dividend of 15p per share.

(c)   Interest on the debentures has not been paid or charged in the accounts for the last six months of the year.

(d)   The stock at the close of business on 31 December 20X3 was valued at cost at £16,224,000.

(e)   The corporation tax charge for the year has been calculated as £4,701,000.

(f)   Land and buildings were revalued during the year. The depreciation charge of £216,000 relating to the buildings has been calculated on the revalued amount and entered in the accounts in the trial balance. The depreciation charge calculated on the original historical cost of the buildings would have been £186,000.

(g)   All of the operations of the business are continuing operations. There were no acquisitions in the year.

TASK 1.2

Draft a profit and loss account for the year ended 31 December 20X3.

TASK 1.3

Prepare a note on historical cost profits and losses as required by FRS 3.

TASK 1.4

Draft a letter to the directors of Kentish Ltd outlining the main types of share capital and their characteristics.

Part C

You should spend about 30 minutes on this part.

Data

You are presented with the following information for Evans Ltd.

EVANS LIMITED
PROFIT AND LOSS ACCOUNT FOR THE YEAR ENDED 31 OCTOBER 20X1

	£'000
Sales	2,000
Cost of goods sold	(1,350)
Gross profit	650
Distribution costs	(99)
Administrative expenses	(120)
Operating profit	431
Gain on disposal of fixed assets	10
Dividend received	12
Interest paid	(35)
Profit before taxation	418
Tax on profit on ordinary activities	(125)
Net profit on ordinary activities after taxation	293
Less proposed dividends	(90)
Retained profit for the financial year	203
Profit and loss account at 31 October 20X0	70
Profit and loss account at 31 October 20X1	273

EVANS LIMITED
BALANCE SHEETS AS AT 31 OCTOBER

	20X0		20X1	
	£'000	£'000	£'000	£'000
Fixed assets				
Furniture at cost	700		900	
Less depreciation	200		270	
		500		630
Vehicles at cost	820		890	
Less depreciation	310		340	
		510		550
Investments, at cost		80		155
		1,090		1,335
Current assets				
Stock	505		486	
Debtors	577		790	
Cash and bank	10		2	
	1,092		1,278	
Current liabilities				
Creditors	546		560	
Taxation	106		125	
Proposed dividends	40		90	
	692		775	
Net current assets		400		503
		1,490		1,838
12% debentures		150		50
		1,340		1,788
Capital and reserves				
Ordinary share capital		1,000		1,200
Share premium		270		315
Profit and loss account		70		273
		1,340		1,788

Additional information for the year ended 31 October 20X1

(a) Vehicles which had cost £155,000 were sold during the year when their net book value was £65,000.

(b) There were no prepaid or accrued expenses at the beginning or end of the year.

TASK 1.5

(a) Prepare a cash flow statement for Evans Ltd for the year ended 31 October 20X1. State the accounting standard you have applied, and show any additional notes and reconciliations required.

(b) What are the advantages of cash flow statements?

Section 2

You should spend about 55 minutes on this section.

Part A

You should spend about 40 minutes on this part.

Data

Michael Beacham has been asked to lend money to Goodall Ltd for a period of three years. He employed a financial adviser to advise him whether to make a loan to the company. The financial adviser has obtained the financial statements of the company for the past two years, calculated some ratios and found the industry averages. However, she was unable to complete her report. Michael has asked you to analyse the ratios and to advise him on whether he should make a loan to Goodall Ltd. The ratios are set out below.

	20X2	20X1	Industry average
Gearing ratio	67%	58%	41%
Interest cover	1.2	2.3	4.6
Quick ratio/acid test	0.5	0.8	1.1
Return on equity	9%	13%	19%

TASK 2.1

Write a report for Michael Beacham that includes the following.

(a)   An explanation of the meaning of each ratio

(b)   A comment on Goodall Ltd's financial position and the performance of the company as shown by the ratios

(c)   A statement of how the financial position and performance have changed over the two years, and how they compare with the industry average

(d)   A conclusion on whether Michael should lend money to Goodall Ltd. Base your conclusion only on the ratios calculated and the analysis performed

Part B

You should spent about 15 minutes on this part.

Data

The *Statement of Principles for Financial Reporting* says that:

'The objective of financial statements is to provide information about the reporting entity's financial performance and financial position that is useful to a wide range of users for assessing the stewardship of the entity's management and for making economic decisions.'

It also says:

'The elements of the financial statements are:

(a)	Assets
(b)	Liabilities
(c)	Ownership interest
(d)	Gains
(e)	Losses
(f)	Contribution from owners
(g)	Distribution to owners.'

TASK 2.2

(a) Explain how the objective of financial statements has been met in the situation set out in Part A above.

(b)   (i)   In which primary financial statement are 'assets', 'liabilities' and 'ownership interest' shown?

    (ii)   How are they related to each other in that statement?

(c)   What is meant by 'gains' and 'losses' and in which primary financial statements are they shown?

DECEMBER 2002 EXAM PAPER

TECHNICIAN STAGE – NVQ4

Unit 11

Drafting Financial Statements
(Accounting Practice, Industry and Commerce)

Time allowed – 3 hours plus 15 minutes' reading time

BPP note

This exam has been amended to reflect the form and content of the new standards.

DO NOT OPEN THIS PAPER UNTIL YOU ARE READY TO START
UNDER EXAM CONDITIONS

COVERAGE OF PERFORMANCE CRITERIA

All Unit 11 performance criteria are covered in this exam.

INSTRUCTIONS

This examination paper is in TWO sections.

You have to show competence in BOTH sections.

You should therefore attempt and aim to complete EVERY task in BOTH sections.

You should spend about 125 minutes on Section 1 and 55 minutes on Section 2.

You are allowed **three hours** to complete your work.

Write your answers in the answer booklet provided. If you require additional answer pages, ask the person in charge.

You may pull apart and rearrange your booklets if you wish to do so, but you must put them back in their original order before handing them in.

Correcting fluid may be used but should be used in moderation. Errors should be crossed out neatly and clearly. You should write in blue or black ink, not pencil.

A high level of accuracy is required. Check your work carefully before handing it in.

A full answer to this exam is given on page 167 of this Kit.

Section 1

You should spend about 125 minuets on this section.

This section is in three parts.

Part A

You should spend about 45 minutes on this part.

Data

Spice Ltd's capital consists of 2,000,000 ordinary shares of £1 each. On 1 November 20X1 Sugar plc acquired 80% of the issued ordinary share capital of Spice Ltd for £2,100,000. At that time, the retained profits of Spice Ltd were £125,000. The summarised profit and loss accounts of the two companies for the year ended 31 October 20X2 are as follows.

	Sugar plc £'000	Spice Ltd £'000
Turnover	2,800	1,000
Cost of sales	1,650	550
Gross profit	1,150	450
Distribution costs	500	190
Administrative expenses	300	120
Operating profit	350	140
Dividend from Spice Ltd	40	-
Profit on ordinary activities before taxation	390	140
Tax on profit on ordinary activities	175	35
Profit on ordinary activities after taxation	215	105
Proposed ordinary dividends	100	50
Retained profit for the year	115	55
Retained profit brought forward	275	150
Retained profit carried forward	390	205

The following information is also available.

(a) Goodwill is amortised over five years.

(b) Sugar plc sold goods costing £85,000 to Spice Ltd for £165,000 during the year ended 31 October 20X2. At 31 October 20X2, 40% of these goods remained in Spice Ltd's stocks.

TASK 1.1

Prepare the consolidated profit and loss account for Sugar plc for the year ended 31 October 20X2. Your consolidated profit and loss account should include the group's retained profit brought forward and carried forward. Disclosure notes are not required.

Part B

You should spend about 50 minutes on this part.

Data

The Chief Accountant of Quine Ltd has asked you to help prepare the financial statements for the year ended 30 September 20X2. The trial balance of the company as at 30 September 20X2 is set out below.

QUINE LIMITED
TRIAL BALANCE AS AT 30 SEPTEMBER 20X2

	Debit £'000	Credit £'000
Ordinary share capital		3,000
Interest	200	
Trade debtors	1,802	
Interim dividend	600	
Long-term loan		2,500
Distribution costs	980	
Administrative expenses	461	
Sales		9,716
Profit and loss account		2,625
Cash at bank	103	
Accruals		105
Prepayments	84	
Share premium		500
Land: cost	2,800	
Buildings: cost	1,480	
Fixtures and fittings: cost	645	
Motor vehicles: cost	1,632	
Office equipment cost	447	
Buildings: accumulated depreciation		702
Fixtures and fittings: accumulated depreciation		317
Motor vehicles: accumulated depreciation		903
Office and equipment: accumulated depreciation		182
Stock as at 1 October 20X1	2,003	
Trade creditors		1,309
Purchases	7,854	
Provision for doubtful debts		72
Capitalised development expenditure	840	
	21,931	21,931

Further information

(a) The authorised share capital of the company, all of which has been issued, consists of ordinary shares with a nominal value of £1.

(b) The company paid an interim dividend of 20p per share during the year but has not provided for the proposed final dividend of 10p per share.

(c) The stock at the close of business on 30 September 20X2 was valued at cost at £2,382,000.

(d) The corporation tax charge for the year has been calculated as £548,000. This has not yet been provided.

(e) The land has been revalued by professional valuers at £3,200,000. The revaluation is to be included in the financial statements for the year ended 30 September 20X2.

TASK 1.2

Make any adjustments required as a result of the further information provided, and draft a balance sheet for Quine Ltd as at 30 September 20X2.

Notes

(a) You are not required to produce notes to the accounts.

(b) You must show any workings relevant to understanding your calculation of figures appearing in the financial statements.

(c) You are not required to produce journal entries for any adjustments required to the figures in the extended trial balance.

Data

The Chief Accountant of Quine Ltd has heard that SSAP 2 has been superseded by FRS 18. He knows that FRS 18 requires that an entity should adopt accounting policies that enable its financial statements to give a true and fair view. However, he is not sure how this will affect the year end financial statements and has asked you to clarify certain aspects of the accounting standard. He has arranged a meeting with you to discuss these matters.

TASK 1.3

Prepare notes for the meeting covering the following matters.

(a) What accounting requirements should Quine Ltd have in selecting accounting policies according to FRS 18? Are there any circumstances where departure from these requirements is necessary?

(b) What four objectives should be used to assess the appropriateness of any particular accounting policies?

(c) What two concepts are said to play a pervasive role in financial statements and hence in the selection of accounting policies?

Part C

You should spend about 30 minutes on this part.

Data

You are presented with Newton Ltd's summary profit and loss account for the year ended 31 December 20X9 and the balance sheet at the beginning and end of the year.

NEWTON LIMITED
PROFIT AND LOSS ACCOUNT FOR THE YEAR ENDED 31 DECEMBER 20X9

	£'000
Profit on ordinary activities before taxation	2,440
Tax on profit on ordinary activities	895
Profit on ordinary activities after taxation	1,545
Less proposed dividends	80
Retained profit for the financial year	1,465
Profit and loss account at 1 January 20X9	1,090
Profit and loss account at 31 December 20X9	2,555

NEWTON LIMITED
BALANCE SHEETS AS AT

	1 January 20X9		31 December 20X9	
	£'000	£'000	£'000	£'000
Fixed assets				
Cost		6,545		9,563
Depreciation		5,120		6,010
		1,425		3,553
Current assets				
Stock	2,695		4,217	
Debtors	1,740		2,500	
	4,435		6,717	
Current liabilities				
Creditors	2,065		3,290	
Bank overdraft	110		420	
Taxation	400		895	
Proposed dividends	30		80	
	2,605		4,685	
Net current assets		1,830		2,032
		3,255		5,585
Long-term loans		875		1,145
		2,380		4,440
Capital and reserves				
Ordinary share capital		795		1,235
Share premium		495		650
Profit and loss account		1,090		2,555
		2,380		4,440

Notes

(a)   During the year fixed assets were sold for £500,000. They cost £2,500,000 and had a net book value of £750,000.

(b)   Interest paid during the year was £235,000.

(c)   There was no under or over provision for corporation tax in the previous year.

TASK 1.4

Prepare a cash flow statement for Newton Ltd for the year ended 31 December 20X9 in accordance with recognised accounting standards. Present any additional notes or reconciliations required by the accounting standard adopted.

Section 2

You should spend about 55 minutes on this part.

Data

Karel Popper is the Managing Director of Zipps Ltd, a company that distributes clothing accessories. The company wishes to raise a loan to finance the expansion of activities. The bank has asked for information about the company including a copy of the financial statements for the past two years. Karel wants to know how likely it is that the bank would be willing to lend the company money on the basis of the financial position revealed in the financial statements alone. He has asked you to advise him on this matter. He also has some questions about financial accounting and reporting. He has given you the profit and loss accounts of Zipps Ltd and the summarised balance sheets for the past two years. These are set out below.

ZIPPS LIMITED
PROFIT AND LOSS ACCOUNT FOR THE YEAR ENDED 30 SEPTEMBER

	20X2	20X1
	£'000	£'000
Turnover	2,412	2,496
Cost of sales	1,158	1,123
Gross profit	1,254	1,373
Distribution costs	814	651
Administrative expenses	486	452
Operating profit/(loss)	(46)	270
Interest payable and similar charges	104	77
Profit/(loss) on ordinary activities before taxation	(150)	193
Tax on profit on ordinary activities	-	42
Profit for the financial year	(150)	151
Dividends	50	50
Retained profit/(loss) for the financial year	(200)	101

ZIPPS LIMITED
BALANCE SHEETS AS AT 30 SEPTEMBER

	20X2		20X1	
	£'000	£'000	£'000	£'000
Fixed assets		1,220		1,118
Current assets				
Stocks	845		620	
Debtors	402		416	
Cash	183		266	
	1,430		1,302	
Current liabilities				
Trade creditors	650		620	
Net current assets		780		682
		2,000		1,800
Called up share capital:				
Ordinary shares of £1 each		200		200
Profit and loss account		500		700
Long-term loan		1,300		900
		2,000		1,800

TASK 2.1

Prepare a letter for Karel Popper that includes the following.

(a)   A calculation of the following ratios of Zipps Ltd for each of the two years:

(i)   Current ratio
(ii)   Quick ratio/acid test
(iii)   Gearing ratio
(iv)   Interest cover

(b)   An explanation of the meaning of each ratio

(c)   A comment on how each ratio has changed over the two years and how this has affected the liquidity and the financial position of Zipps Ltd

(d)   A brief indication of other ratios that the bank may wish to calculate and why (you do not need to calculate them or comment on them in any way)

(e)   A conclusion, with reasons, as to whether it is likely that the bank will lend the company money based solely on the ratios calculated and their analysis

TASK 2.2

(a)   What sort of information in the financial statements does the ASB's *Statement of Principles for Financial Reporting* say that potential investors are interested in and for what purpose?

(b)   How does stock meet the definition of an asset in the ASB's *Statement of Principles for Financial Reporting*?

AAT
Specimen Exam

AAT SPECIMEN EXAM PAPER - 2003 STANDARDS

NVQ/SVQ in ACCOUNTING, LEVEL 4

UNIT 11

DRAFTING FINANCIAL STATEMENTS (ACCOUNTING PRACTICE, INDUSTRY and COMMERCE) (DFS)

This examination is in TWO sections.

You have to show competence in BOTH sections.

You should therefore attempt and aim to complete EVERY task in BOTH sections.

You should spend about 125 minutes on this section.

This section is in three parts.

SECTION 1

Part A

You should spend about 45 minutes on this part.

Data

You have been asked to assist in the preparation of the consolidated accounts of the Jake Group. Set out below are the balance sheets of Jake Ltd and Dinos Ltd for the year ended 30 September 20X1.

	Jake Limited		Dinos Limited	
	£'000	£'000	£'000	£'000
Tangible fixed assets		18,104		6,802
Investment in Dinos Ltd		5,000		
Current assets	4,852		2,395	
Current liabilities	2,376		547	
Net current assets		2,476		1,848
Long term loan		4,500		1,000
		21,080		7,650
Share capital		5,000		1,000
Share premium		3,000		400
Profit and loss account		13,080		6,250
		21,080		7,650

You are given the following further information.

(a) The share capital of both Jake Ltd and Dinos Ltd consists of ordinary shares of £1 each. There have been no changes to the balances of share capital and share premium during the year. No dividends were paid or proposed by Dinos Ltd during the year.

(b) Jake Ltd acquired 600,000 shares in Dinos Ltd on 30 September 20X0.

(c) At 30 September 20X0 the balance on the profit and loss account of Dinos Ltd was £5,450,000.

(d) The fair value of the fixed assets of Dinos Ltd at 30 September 20X0 was £3,652,000 as compared with their book value of £3, 052,000. The revaluation has not been reflected in the books of Dinos Ltd. (Ignore any depreciation implications.)

(e) Goodwill arising on consolidation is to be amortised using the straight-line method over a period of 10 years.

TASK 1.1

Prepare the consolidated balance sheet of Jake Ltd and its subsidiary undertaking as at 30 September 20X1.

TASK 1.2

Prepare notes for the directors of Jake Ltd to answer the following questions.

(a)   What would be the accounting treatment of the goodwill if, instead of having a useful life of 20 years, the goodwill was regarded as having an indefinite useful economic life?

(b)   If so, what would be the appropriate accounting treatment?

Your answer should make reference, where relevant, to accounting standards.

Part B

You are advised to spend about 50 minutes on this part.

Data

You have been asked to help prepare the financial statements of Hightink Ltd for the year ended 30 September 20X2. The trial balance of the company as at 30 September 20X2 is below.

HIGHTINK LIMITED
TRIAL BALANCE AS AT 30 SEPTEMBER 20X2

	Debit £'000	Credit £'000
Interest	240	
Distribution costs	6,852	
Administration expenses	3,378	
Trade debtors	5,455	
Trade creditors		2,363
Interim dividend	400	
Ordinary share capital		4,000
Sales		31,710
Long term loan		6,000
Land: cost	5,000	
Buildings: cost	3,832	
Fixtures and fittings: cost	2,057	
Motor vehicles: cost	3,524	
Office equipment: cost	2,228	
Purchases	15,525	
Cash at bank	304	
Profit and loss account		6,217
Stock as at 1 October 20X1	6,531	
Share premium		2,000
Buildings: accumulated depreciation		564
Fixtures and fittings: accumulated depreciation		726
Motor vehicles: accumulated depreciation		1,283
Office equipment: accumulated depreciation		463
	55,326	55,326

Further information

(a) The authorised share capital of the company, all of which has been issued, consists of ordinary shares with a nominal value of £1.

(b) The company paid an interim dividend of 10p per share during the year but has not provided for the proposed final dividend of 15p per share.

(c) The stock at the close of business on 30 September 20X2 was valued at cost at £7,878,000.

(d)   The corporation tax charge for the year has been calculated as £1,920,000.

(e)   Credit sales relating to October 20X2 amounting to £204,000 had incorrectly been entered into the accounts in September 20X2.

(f)   Interest on the long term loan has been paid for six months of the year. No adjustment has been made for the interest due for the final six months of the year. Interest is charged on the loan at a rate of 8% per annum.

(g)   On 21 October 20X2 there was a fire at the company's premises that destroyed fixed assets and stocks. The losses from the fire amounted to £487,000 and they were not covered by the company's insurance. This amount is considered by the directors to constitute a material loss to the company.

TASK 1.3

Make the necessary journal entries for the year ended 30 September 20X2 as a result of the further information given above. Dates and narratives are not required.

Notes

1   You must show any workings relevant to these adjustments.
2   Ignore the effect of these adjustments on the tax charge for the year given above.

TASK 1.4

Making any adjustments required as a result of the further information provided, draft a profit and loss account for the year ending 30 September 20X2 for Hightink Ltd.

TASK 1.5

Prepare a memo for the directors of Hightink Ltd to cover the following matters.

(a)   Explain what is meant by a 'post balance sheet event'.

(b)   Distinguish between a post balance sheet event that is an 'adjusting event' and one that is a 'non-adjusting event'.

(c)   Explain your treatment of the losses that arose from the fire on the company's premises on 21 October 20X2.

Part C

You are advised to spend about 30 minutes on this part.

Data

You have been asked to prepare a cash flow statement for Stringberg Ltd for the year ended 31 March 20X1. The profit and loss account and balance sheets of Stringberg Ltd are set out below.

STRINGBERG LIMITED
PROFIT AND LOSS ACCOUNT FOR THE YEAR ENDED 31 MARCH 20X1

	£'000
Turnover	9,047
Cost of sales	4,939
Gross profit	4,108
Profit on the sale of fixed assets	93
Distribution costs	1,013
Administrative expenses	722
Profit on ordinary activities before interest	2,466
Interest paid and similar charges	243
Profit on ordinary activities before taxation	2,223
Tax on profit on ordinary activities	509
Profit for the financial year	1,714
Dividends	630
Retained profit for the financial year	1,084

STRINGBERG LIMITED
BALANCE SHEETS AS AT 31 MARCH

	20X1		20X0	
	£'000	£'000	£'000	£'000
Fixed assets		5,366		4,075
Current assets				
Stocks	3,016		2,284	
Trade debtors	1,508		1,394	
Cash	23		–	
	4,547		3,678	
Current liabilities				
Trade creditors	1,372		930	
Dividends payable	420		380	
Taxation	509		492	
Bank overdraft	–		137	
	2,301		1,939	
Net current assets		2,246		1,739
Long term loan		(3,038)		(3,324)
		4,574		2,490

	20X1	20X0
	£'000	£'000
Capital and reserves		
Called up share capital	2,500	1,900
Share premium	400	–
Profit and loss account	1,674	590
	4,574	2,490

Further information

(a) A fixed asset costing £363,000 with accumulated depreciation of £173,000 was sold during the year. The total depreciation charge for the year was £505,000.

(b) All sales and purchases were on credit. Other expenses were paid for in cash.

TASK 1.6

Prepare a reconciliation of operating profit to net cash flows from operating activities for Stringberg Ltd for the year ended 31 March 20X1.

TASK 1.7

Prepare a cash flow statement for Stringberg Ltd for the year ended 31 March 20X1 in accordance with the requirements of FRS 1 (revised).

SECTION 2

You are advised to spend approximately 55 minutes on this section.

Data

Jake Matease plans to invest in Fauve Ltd. This is a chain of retail outlets. He is going to meet the managing directors of Fauve Ltd to discus the profitability of the company. To prepare for the meeting he has asked you to comment on the change in profitability and the return on capital of the company. He also has some questions about the balance sheet of the company. He has given you the profit and loss accounts of Fauve Ltd and the summarised balance sheets for the last two years.

FAUVE LIMITED
SUMMARY PROFIT AND LOSS ACCOUNTS
FOR THE YEAR ENDED 30 SEPTEMBER

	20X1	20X0
	£'000	£'000
Turnover	4,315	2,973
Cost of sales	1,510	1,189
Gross profit	2,805	1,784
Distribution costs	983	780
Administrative expenses	571	380
Operating profit	1,251	624
Interest paid and similar charges	45	27
Profit on ordinary activities before taxation	1,206	597
Tax on profit on ordinary activities	338	167
Profit for the financial year	868	430
Dividends	340	300
Retained profit for the financial year	528	130

FAUVE LIMITED
BALANCE SHEETS AS AT 30 SEPTEMBER

	20X1		20X0	
	£'000	£'000	£'000	£'000
Fixed assets		6,663		4,761
Current assets	3,503		2,031	
Current liabilities	1,736		1,387	
Net current assets		1,767		644
Long-term loam		(500)		(300)
		7,930		5,105
Called up share capital: ordinary shares of £1 each		4,000		1,703
Profit and loss account		3,930		3,402
		7,930		5,105

TASK 2.1

Prepare a report for Jake Matease that includes the following.

(a)   A calculation of the following ratios of Fauve Ltd for each of the two years:

(i)   Return on capital employed
(ii)   Net profit percentage
(iii) Gross profit percentage
(iv)   Asset turnover

(b)   An explanation of the meaning of each ratio and a comment on the performance of Fauve Ltd a shown by each of the ratios

(c)   A conclusion on how the overall performance has changed over the two years

TASK 2.2

Prepare notes for a meeting with Jack Matease that answers the following questions relating to the balance sheet of Fauve Ltd.

(a)   Why is the plant and machinery included in the fixed assets of the company classified as an 'asset' of the business?

(b)   Why is the bank loan classified as a 'liability' of the business?

(c)   (i)   Why is the final figure of 'retained profit for the year' in the profit and loss account not the same figure that appears in the balance for the profit and loss account on the balance sheet of the company?

(i)   Is there any connection between the two figures?

Answers to Practice Activities

Chapters 1 and 2 Introduction; Accounting conventions

1 Objectives

(a) The ASB *Statement of Principles* (Chapter 1) sets out the objectives of financial reporting.

Financial reporting has the objectives of providing information regarding the financial position, performance and financial adaptability of an entity.

The provision of such information will enable the various users of financial statements to take better informed decisions on economic matters such as investment planning .

The financial reporting package is also designed to provide information regarding the stewardship activities of the managers of a business to its owners. For limited companies, such information is required by law to be produced in a form prescribed by the Companies Act.

(b) The user groups identified by the ASB *Statement of Principles* were as follows.

(i)   Public
(ii)   Investors
(iii) Lenders
(iv)   Government and other agencies
(v)   Employees
(vi)   The Suppliers and other creditors
(vii) Customers

(c) The information needs of each group are as follows.

Investors need data to enable investment decisions (buy, sell, hold) to be taken. The provision of information regarding stewardship is also important.

Lenders will need to know the financial position of a business in order to judge security and the ability of the business to repay the interest or capital. Decisions will also be needed regarding the ability of a business to handle an increased level of borrowings.

The government will need information to compile national statistics, to determine taxation liabilities and to assess applications for financial support received from companies. The compilation of data of regarding national economic performance will be helped by having a financial reporting package presented in a consistent manner by a variety of contributors.

Employees will need information to take decisions regarding employment prospects, stability of employers and to enable wage demands to be formulated. Bonus payments are also usually linked to reported performance levels

The public will want to know the relationship of the reporting entity with the community within which it operates, eg its contribution to the local economy. Increasingly, environmental issues are of concern as well.

Suppliers will need information in order to assess requests for lines of trade credit and the ability of their creditors to pay up on time.

Customers will need reassurance that an entity is sufficiently stable to satisfy their order on time and to specification. They will also use the reporting package to help to select a supplier.

(d)   This a very wide ranging question.

Clearly no single reporting package can completely meet all the diverse needs discussed above, so what has emerged is something of a compromise. Traditionally, the view has been that provided the needs of shareholders are met, then the reporting package will also have gone a long way towards satisfying other users needs.

However, recent reporting developments such as summary financial statements, employee reports and environmental reports have gone some way to meeting the needs of specific user groups and this trend will no doubt continue.

Financial reporting is gradually moving towards satisfying the information needs of other user groups. However, financial reports are becoming ever more complex and some would say that they are increasingly difficult for non financially orientated users to deal with.

The final point is that the financial reporting package is essentially historical and is generally of only limited use in assessing the current or future status of an entity unless used in conjunction with other sources of information.

2 Accounting equation

(a)   Each of the items in the accounting equation is defined in the ASB's *Statement of Principles*.

(i)   *Assets* are 'rights or other access to future economic benefits controlled by an entity as a result of past transactions or events'.

(ii)   *Liabilities* are 'obligations of an entity to transfer economic benefits as a result of past transactions or events'.

(iii)   *Ownership interest* is the residual amount found by deducting all of the entity's liabilities from all of the entity's assets.

(b)   Transaction 1 would increase stock, an asset, by £120 and also increase creditors, a liability, by £120.

Transaction 2 would decrease the asset stock by £120, but increase the asset cash by £180. Thus there would be a net increase in assets of £60. In the other half of the balance sheet, ownership interest would increase by £60, being the profit made on the sale.

(c)   The accounting equation after the two transactions would be:

ASSETS	LESS	LIABILITIES	=	OWNERSHIP INTEREST
£1,380		£920		£460

(d)   PROFIT AND LOSS ACCOUNT

	£
Sales	180
Cost of sales	120
	60

(e)   There are a number of users who might be interested in a profit and loss account. The *Statement of Principles* identifies, amongst others, shareholders, lenders, employees, suppliers and customers. Shareholders will be particularly interested in the profit and loss account, because they will want to know whether management's stewardship of the money they have invested has been effective. The profit and loss account shows how the increase (or decrease) in ownership interest has been made as a result of the company's operations. It is also a useful tool in making comparisons of the company's performance with the performance of previous accounting periods or with other companies in the same sector.

3 Objective and elements

(a)   The objective of financial statements has been set out in the ASB's *Statement of Principles* as follows.

'To provide information about the financial position, performance and financial adaptability of an enterprise that is useful to a wide range of users for assessing the stewardship of management and for making economic decisions.'

Whether financial statements meet this objective in all cases is debatable.

(b)   One of the financial statements, the balance sheet, exists to provide information about the company's financial position, for example what it owns (assets) and what it owes (liabilities). The balance sheet also gives an indication of financial adaptability, for example whether the company has sufficient cash to settle debts if required. Information about financial performance is given in the profit and loss account.

(c)   The elements of financial statements are identified in Chapter 4 of the *Statement of Principles* as follows.

(i)   Assets   (vi)   Gains
(ii)   Liabilities   (vii)   Losses
(iii)   Ownership interest   (viii) Contributions from owners
(iv)   Income   (ix)   Distributions to owners
(v)   Expenditure

(d)   The elements of financial statements are interrelated in the profit and loss account and balance sheet by means of the accounting equation:

Assets – Liabilities = Ownership interest

(Ownership interest is also, in the accounts of a profit-making organisation, known as 'capital'.)

The change in ownership interest is equal to the profit for the accounting period plus contributions from owners (capital introduced) less distributions to owners (drawings and dividends).

Profit is, in effect, gains less losses. Some gains and losses are recorded in the profit and loss account and others in the statement of total recognised gains and losses, but the relationship of the elements is the same.

4 Assets and liabilities

(a) **Assets** are defined in the ASB's *Statement of Principles* as 'rights or other access to future economic benefits controlled by an entity as a result of past transactions or events'. Each part of this definition can be applied to the plant and machinery as follows.

    (i) The company has rights and access to any **future economic benefits** generated by the products manufactured by the plant and machinery.

    (ii) The company **controls** the plant and machinery and has right to use it.

    (iii) There has been a **past transaction,** namely the purchase of the plant and machinery.

(b) **Liabilities** are also defined by the *Statement of Principles.* The definition is, 'obligations of an entity to **transfer economic benefits** as a result of past transaction or events'. This definition can be applied to the bank loan as follows.

    (i) The entity has an **obligation to transfer economic benefits** in the future in that the loan must be repaid and interest must be paid on the loan.

    (ii) The obligation arose as a result of a **past transaction**, namely the receipt of money from the bank.

(c)   (i) The figure of 'retained profit for the year' relates only to the current year. The retained profit figure in the balance sheet represents the accumulated profits from previous years insofar as they have not been distributed as dividends.

    (ii) The two are connected. The profit for the year in the profit and loss account is added to the profits brought forward from previous years. The total is the retained profits carried forward which is shown in the balance sheet.

5 Balancing

(a) The accounting equation is as follows.

ASSETS LESS LIABILITIES = OWNERSHIP INTEREST

In the balance sheet of a not-for-profit organisation, such as a club, you will find an accumulated fund. This will be made up of capital introduced and accumulated surpluses of income over expenditure and is to be applied to further the organisation's aims.

In the balance sheet of a company, the ownership interest section consists of share capital (originally paid in by the owners) and reserves (profits made by the company and owed to the owners). These are the equivalent of the 'funds' balances in not-for-profit organisations.

(b)   (i) **Suppliers** may be interested in the financial statements in order to decide whether to carry on supplying goods on credit (by looking at the liquidity position).

    (ii) **Potential** *investors* may need this information to decide whether or not they should invest in the company.

    (iii) **The bank** may wish to decide whether to continue an overdraft facility or grant a loan by assessing profitability and liquidity.

Chapters 3 and 4 Regulation

6 Accounting standards

The structure of the standard setting process in the UK is as follows.

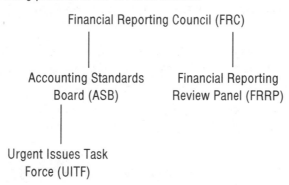

The FRC overseas the standard-setting process. It guides the ASB and the FRRP and appoints members and arranges funding. It also gives guidance to the ASB on matters of policy and on programmes of work, and, in addition gives advice to government on how accounting legislation might be improved.

The ASB is the body responsible for setting accounting standards, now called financial reporting standards or FRSs. There is a lengthy consultation procedure, involving the issue of discussion drafts and financial reporting exposure drafts (FREDs), which must be undertaken before an FRS can be issued.

The UITF is a sub-committee of the ASB whose function it is to tackle urgent matters not covered by existing standards, where, given the urgency of the matter, the normal standard-setting procedure would be too time consuming.

The FRRP is concerned with the examination and questioning of departures from accounting standards by large companies. Where accounts depart from accounting standards, the FRRP needs to determine whether they still give a true and fair view. Generally most referrals are resolved by discussion, but failing that, the Panel has the power to apply to the court for revision of the accounts.

Chapters 5 to 7 Fixed assets and stocks

7 Depreciation

(a) Where fixed assets are disposed of for an amount which is greater or less than their book value, the surplus or deficiency should be reflected in the results of the year and disclosed separately if material. Following the provisions of FRS 3 *Reporting financial performance,* a material amount should be disclosed on the face of the profit and loss account.

(b) A change from one method of providing depreciation to another is permissible only on the grounds that the new method will give a fairer presentation of the results and of the financial position. In these circumstances the unamortised cost of the asset should be written off over the remaining useful life on the new basis commencing with the period in which the change is made. The effect should be disclosed in the year of change, if material.

8 Revaluations

Notes for Board Meeting – Revaluation of Land and Buildings

(a)   A company may adopt a policy of revaluing tangible fixed assets. However, FRS 15 *Tangible fixed assets* states that where such a policy is adopted, it must be applied consistently to all assets of the same class. A class of fixed assets is a category of tangible fixed assets which have a similar nature or function in the company's business.

From this it follows that if the directors decide to adopt a policy of revaluation for land and buildings, they will need to revalue all the land and buildings that the company owns. It will not be permissible to revalue some and not others.

(b)   (i)   According to FRS 15, where an asset is revalued, its carrying amount should be its current value as at the balance sheet date. Current value is the lower of replacement cost and recoverable amount.

(ii)   FRS 15 states that non-specialised properties should be valued on the basis of existing use value.

(iii)   Revaluation gains are recognised in the statement of total recognised gains and losses, except to the extent that they reverse revaluation losses on the same assets, in which case they should be recognised in the profit and loss account.

9 Stocks

(a)   *Cost* is that expenditure which has been incurred in the normal course of business in bringing the product or service to its present location and condition. This expenditure should include:

(i)   Cost of purchase (including import duties, transport and handling costs and any other directly attributable costs, less trade discounts, rebates and subsidies)

(ii)   Any costs of conversion appropriate to that location and condition (including direct labour and expenses, and attributable production overheads)

(b)   *Net realisable value* is the actual or estimated selling price (net of trade but before settlement discounts) less:

(i)   All further costs to completion
(ii)   All costs to be incurred in marketing, selling and distributing

10 SSAP 13

Tutorial note. Parts (a) and (b) here are straightforward. However, part (c) may have caused candidates problems. If a question involves a SSAP or FRS, you will almost certainly be required to demonstrate understanding as well as rote learning.

(a)   SSAP 13 recognises three categories of research and development expenditure.

   (i)   *Pure or basic research* is directed primarily towards the advancement of knowledge.

   (ii)   *Applied research* is directed towards exploiting pure research, for a specific aim or objective, other than work defined as development.

   (iii)   *Development expenditure* is directed towards the introduction or improvement of specific products or processes.

(b)   Only development expenditure may be capitalised and then only if it satisfies all of the following conditions.

   (i)   There is a clearly defined project.

   (ii)   The relevant expenditure is clearly and separately identifiable.

   (iii)   The project is considered to be technically, environmentally and commercially feasible.

   (iv)   The expenditure (including any future expenditure) is expected to be more than recoverable from the future revenues that will flow from the project.

   (v)   Adequate physical and human resources exist to complete the project.

   (vi)   Management has made a decision to allocate the necessary resources to the project.

(c)   The need for the standard arose from a concern that some companies were capitalising large amounts of R&D that were unlikely to be recovered from future revenues. This practice inflated the net assets of companies who followed it and made it difficult to compare their accounts with those of companies that wrote off their R&D expenditure. Equally, other companies were writing off large amounts of expenditure which could have been deferred. The standard thus imposed consistency and comparability.

The particular case that it is thought may have prompted the ASC to act was that of Rolls-Royce who went bankrupt and had to be nationalised at a time when it was carrying very large sums in its balance sheet in respect of capitalised R&D costs for the RB 211 aero engine.

11 Goodwill

NOTE TO THE DIRECTORS – TREATMENT OF GOODWILL

(a)   Both positive purchased goodwill and purchased intangible assets should initially be capitalised and classed as an asset at cost.

(b)   Inherent (non-purchased) goodwill should not be capitalised.

(c)   When intangible assets are acquired as part of a takeover they should be capitalised separately from goodwill if their fair value can be reliably measured. If this is not possible, then they should be subsumed into goodwill.

(d)   If, after stringently testing the fair values of the assets for impairment, negative goodwill arises this should be shown on the balance sheet separately and immediately below positive goodwill.

(e)   Goodwill and intangible assets should be amortised on a systematic basis over their useful economic lives. If it is considered that the economic life is infinite no amortisation is needed.

(f)   It is presumed that intangibles (including goodwill) have a life of less than 20 years but this is rebuttable. This, however, puts the responsibility on the reporting entity to demonstrate that not only does the asset have an extended life but that its value is capable of an annual impairment review.

(g)   In all cases the economic life should be reviewed annually.

Chapter 8 Reporting financial performance

12 Jenny

(a)   ANGLE LIMITED
        STATEMENT OF TOTAL RECOGNISED GAINS AND LOSSES
        FOR THE YEAR ENDED 31 MARCH 20X1

	£'000
Profit for the financial year	1,145
Unrealised surplus on revaluation of properties	500
Total gains and losses recognised since last annual report	1,645

(b)   (i)   An acquisition is an operation of the reporting entity that is acquired during the period.

A discontinued operation is one which meets four conditions.

(1)   The sale or termination must be completed before the earlier of three months after the year end or the date the financial statements are approved.

(2)   The former activity must have ceased permanently.

(3)   The sale or termination has a material effect on the nature and focus of the entity's operations and represents a material reduction in its operating facilities.

(4)   The assets, liabilities, results of operations and activities are clearly distinguishable.

(ii)   The distinction between acquisitions, continuing operations and discontinued operations enables the user of accounts to make a better judgement of the company's performance, both past and future. For example, if a company did not appear to be very profitable, but the profit and loss account thus analysed showed that a poor performing division had been closed during the year, a user might be able to predict more favourable results for the future. Equally, if good performance is due to an acquisition, this needs to be shown separately, rather than merged with the rest of the company's results. Furthermore an acquisition must be ignored when comparing this year's results with those of previous years, so that like is compared with like.

Chapters 3 to 9 Limited company scenario questions

13 Fun

(a)   The journal entries required are as follows.

	Debit £'000	Credit £'000
Dividends (p&l) (£8,000,000 × 0.1)	800	
Dividends payable		800
Corporation tax (p&l)	972	
Corporation tax (creditor)		972
Interest charge (p&l) (8% × £3,600,000 × 1/12)	24	
Accruals		24

(b)   FUN LIMITED
PROFIT AND LOSS ACCOUNT FOR THE YEAR ENDED 31 SEPTEMBER 20X8

	£'000
Turnover (continuing operations) (W1)	14,363
Cost of sales (W2)	6,464
Gross profit	7,899
Distribution costs	2,669
Administrative expenses	2,042
Operating profit (continuing operations)	3,188
Interest payable and similar charges (300+24)	324
Profit on ordinary activities before taxation	2,864
Tax on profit on ordinary activities	972
Profit on ordinary activities after taxation	1,892
Dividends (480+800)	1,280
Retained profit for the financial year	612

Workings

1   *Turnover*

	£'000
Sales	14,595
Returns inwards	(232)
	14,363

2 *Cost of sales*

	£'000
Opening stock	1,893
Purchases	6,671
Carriage inwards	87
Returns outwards	(146)
Closing stock	(2,041)
	6,464

(c) **NOTES FOR BOARD MEETING DEALING WITH ACCOUNTING MATTERS**

(i) A share premium arises when a company sells shares for a price which is higher than the nominal value. By 'premium' is meant the difference between the issue price of the share and its nominal value. For example, if a share with a nominal value of £1 was issued for £1.20, then the accounting entries would be:

DEBIT	Cash	£1.20	
CREDIT	Share capital		£1.00
CREDIT	Share premium		£0.20

The revaluation reserve arose because at some point an asset was revalued. The balance represents the excess of the fair value of the asset over its net value. For example, if the asset had a net book value of £600,000, and its market value was £950,000, the accounting entries would be:

DEBIT	Fixed asset	£350,000	
CREDIT	Revaluation reserve		£350,000

(ii) It is by no means certain that a leased asset can be kept off the balance sheet. The accounting treatment of leased assets is governed by SSAP 21 *Accounting for leases and hire purchase contracts.*

The correct treatment depends on whether the lease is a finance lease or an operating lease. SSAP 21 defines a finance lease as a lease which transfers substantially all the risks and rewards of ownership of an asset to the lessee. An operating lease is a lease other than a finance lease.

If the lease is a finance lease, it should be recorded in Fun Ltd's balance sheet as a asset and as an obligation to pay future rentals. The amount recorded should be the present value of the minimum lease payments derived by discounting them at the interest rate implicit in the lease.

If, however, the lease is an operating lease, the asset belongs to the lessor, and so is not shown on the balance sheet of Fun Ltd. Rentals are charged to the profit and loss account, but future rentals are not shown as a liability on the balance sheet of Fun Ltd.

14 Franco

				£	£
(a)	(i)	DEBIT	Taxation charge	110,000	
		CREDIT	Taxation payable		110,000
		Being taxation charge for the year			
	(ii)	DEBIT	Motor expenses	10,000	
		DEBIT	Wages	2,000	
		CREDIT	General expenses		12,000
	(iii)	DEBIT	Final dividend (appropriation account) (72 – 4 – 30)	38,000	
		DEBIT	Preference dividend (appropriation account)	4,000	
		CREDIT	Dividends proposed		42,000
	(iv)	DEBIT	Loan interest (P&L)	2,000	
		CREDIT	Interest payable		2,000
	(v)	DEBIT	Audit fees (P&L)	9,000	
		CREDIT	Accruals		9,000
	(vi)	No adjustment is needed			
	(vii)	No adjustment is needed			
	(viii)	No adjustment is needed			
	(ix)	No adjustment is needed			
	(x)	No adjustment is needed			

(b) FRANCO LIMITED
PROFIT AND LOSS ACCOUNT FOR THE YEAR ENDED 31 MARCH 20X5

	£'000
Turnover	
Continuing operations	2,460
Cost of sales	999
Gross profit	1,461
Distribution costs	416
Administrative expenses	341
Operating profit	
Continuing operations	704
Interest payable and similar charges	2
Profit on ordinary activities before taxation	702
Tax on profit on ordinary activities	110
Profit on ordinary activities after taxation	592
Dividends	72
Retained profit for the financial year	520

FRANCO LIMITED
BALANCE SHEET AS AT MARCH 20X5

	£'000	£'000
Fixed assets		608
Current assets		
Stocks	225	
Debtors	447	
Cash at bank and in hand	7	
	679	
Creditors: amounts falling due within one year	337	
		342
Total assets less current liabilities		950
Creditors: amounts falling due after more than one year		
Long term loan		20
		930
Capital and reserves		
Called up share capital		250
Profit and loss account		680
		930

Workings

1   *Turnover*

	£'000
Per ETB	2,470
Less returns inwards	10
	2,460

2   *Cost of sales*

Opening stocks	215
Purchases	1,000
Plus carriage inwards	14
Less returns outwards	5
	1,224
Less closing stocks	225
	999

3   *Distribution costs and administrative expenses*

		Administrative expenses	Distribution costs
		£	£
Depreciation:	buildings	3,000	1,000
	fixtures and fittings	4,000	1,000
	motor vehicles	2,000	8,000
	office	1,000	–
Insurance (75/25)		9,000	3,000
Rates		10,000	10,000
Light and heat		18,000	18,000
Audit		9,000	–
Advertising		–	95,000
Increase in provision for doubtful debts		3,000	–
General expenses (135 – 12)		100,000	23,000
Motor expenses (27 + 10)		10,000	27,000
Directors' emoluments		68,000	30,000
Salaries and wages (400 – 98 + 2)		104,000	200,000
		341,000	416,000

4   *Debtors*

	£'000
Trade debtors	450
Less provision for doubtful debts	(9)
	441
Prepayments	6
	447

5   *Fixed assets*

	Cost	Accum depn	Net book value
	£'000	£'000	£'000
Land and buildings	575	24	551
Fixtures and fittings	35	23	12
Motor vehicles	94	64	30
Office equipment	20	5	15
	724	116	608

6   *Creditors: amounts falling due within one year*

	£'000
Trade creditors	170
Corporation tax payable	110
Dividends proposed	42
Accruals (4 + 9)	13
Interest payable	2
	337

7   *Share capital*

		£'000
400,000 ordinary shares of 50p		200
50,000 preference shares of £1		50
		250

8   *Profit and loss account*

	£'000
As at 1 April 20X4	160
Retained profit for the year	520
As at 31 March 20X5	680

(c)   REPORT

To: The Directors
       Franco Ltd

From: Accounting Technician   Date: 5 April 20X5

Stock valuation and filing exemptions

(i)   *Stock valuation*

SSAP 9 states that stocks must be valued at the lower of cost and net realisable value.

Cost is that expenditure which has been incurred in the normal course of business in bringing the product or service to its present location and condition. This expenditure should include:

(1)   Cost of purchase (including import duties, transport and handling costs and any other directly attributable costs, less trade discounts, rebates and subsidies)

(2)   Any costs of conversion appropriate to that location and condition, including direct labour and expenses and attributable production overheads

Net realisable value is the actual or estimated selling price (net of trade but before settlement discounts) less:

(1)   All further costs to completion
(2)   All costs to be incurred in marketing, selling and distributing

Comparison of cost and net realisable value should be made for each item or category of stock separately rather than comparing total cost with total NRV.

(ii)   *Filing exemptions*

Small and medium-sized companies are allowed certain 'filing exemptions': the accounts they lodge with the registrar of companies, and which are available for public inspection need not contain all the information which must be published by large companies.

A company qualifies as a *small* company in a particular financial year, if, for that year, at least two out of the following three limits are not exceeded.

Turnover	*Balance sheet total*	*Average number of employees*
£2.8 million	£1.4 million	50

For a medium sized company, the conditions (at least two of which must be satisfied) are as follows.

Turnover	Balance sheet total	Average number of employees
≤ £11.2 million	≤ £5.6 million	≤ 250

Small companies may file an abbreviated balance sheet showing only the items which, in the statutory format, are denoted by a letter or roman number. No profit and loss account, directors' report or details of directors' emoluments need be filed, and only certain of the notes to the accounts need to be produced.

Medium-sized companies are not required to analyse turnover between class of business or geographical market and the profit and loss account may begin with the figure of gross profit.

Public companies, banking and insurance companies, companies authorised under the Financial Services Act 1986 or members of a group containing any of these may not file abbreviated accounts.

Franco Ltd, by the above definitions, qualifies as a small company.

(d)   MEMORANDUM

To: The Directors
        Franco Ltd

From: Accounting Technician   Date: 3 April 20X5

Accounting treatment

(i)   *Issue of shares at a premium*

When shares are issued at an amount which exceeds their nominal value, the excess must be credited to a share premium account (s 130 CA 85) to which certain restrictions apply. Accordingly the required bookkeeping entries for the shares issued on 10 April will be as follows.

		£	£
DEBIT	Bank	37,500	
CREDIT	Ordinary share capital (50p × 50,000)		25,000
	Share premium (25p × 50,000)		12,500

(ii)   This situation, where a debtor goes into liquidation after the balance sheet date, is one which is specifically mentioned in the appendix to SSAP 17 *Accounting for post balance sheet events* as an 'adjusting post balance sheet event'. Adjusting post balance sheet events are defined in the SSAP as 'post balance sheet events which provide additional evidence of conditions existing at the balance sheet date', and consequently require the relevant amounts in the financial statements to be changed. In this case the debt of £30,000 would need to be written off. The bookkeeping entries would be:

DEBIT	Bad debts	£30,000	
CREDIT	Debtors		£30,000

(iii)   The situation described here is covered by FRS 12 *Provisions, contingent liabilities and contingent assets.* A contingent asset is defined a 'a possible asset that arises from past events and whose existence will only be confirmed by the occurrence of one or more uncertain future events not wholly within the entities control'.

It follows from the above definition that the probable inflow of £25,000 from the legal suit is a 'contingent asset'. FRS 12 states that if a contingent asset is probable, it should be disclosed by way of a note in the financial statements. It cannot be recognised or it would not be a *contingent* asset.

(e)   (i)   'Window dressing' techniques to improve the cash balance might include the following.

     (1)   Personal money is paid into the company bank account just before the year end to boost the cash balance, then withdrawn just after the year end.

     (2)   A large cheque is written against one group company's positive bank balance in favour of another group company with a large overdraft. The cheque is put through at the year end and then cancelled at the beginning of the next year, thus concealing the overdraft in the consolidated balance sheet (where positive and negative bank balances cannot be netted off).

   (ii)   'Window dressing' is not defined in SSAP 17 *Accounting for post balance sheet events.* However, the SSAP does address the problem by requiring disclosure of the reversal or maturity after the year end of transactions entered into before the year end, the substance of which was primarily to alter the appearance of the company's balance sheet.

15 Dowango

(a)				£'000	£'000
(i)	DEBIT	Dividends (500,000 × 6p)		30	
	CREDIT	Dividends payable			30
(ii)	DEBIT	Tax charge (P & L)		211	
	CREDIT	Corporation tax payable			211
(iii)	DEBIT	Interest payable (P & L)		15	
	CREDIT	Accruals (300 × 10% × 6/12)			15
(iv)	DEBIT	Distribution costs		19	
	CREDIT	Accruals			19
(v)	DEBIT	Administrative expenses		8	
	CREDIT	Investments (64 − 56)			8

(b) DOWANGO LIMITED
PROFIT AND LOSS ACCOUNT FOR THE YEAR ENDED 31 MARCH 20X6

	£'000
Turnover (W1)	
Continuing operations	5,352
Cost of sales (W2)	2,910
Gross profit	2,442
Distribution costs (1,104 + 19)	1,123
Administrative expenses (709 + 8)	717
Operating profit	
Continuing operations	602
Interest payable and similar charge (15 + 15)	30
Profit on ordinary activities before taxation	572
Tax on profit on ordinary activities	211
Profit on ordinary activities after tax	361
Dividends (20 + 30)	50
Retained profit for the year	311

DOWNGO LIMITED
BALANCE SHEET AS AT 31 MARCH 20X6

	£'000	£'000
Fixed assets		
Tangible assets (W3)		1,153
Current assets		
Investment	56	
Stock	365	
Debtors (W4)	613	
Cash at bank and in hand	3	
	1,037	
Creditors: amounts falling due within one year (W5)	804	
Net current assets		233
Total assets less current liabilities		1,386
Creditors: amounts falling due after more than one year		300
		1,086
Capital and reserves		
Called up share capital		500
Profit and loss account (275 + 311)		586
		1,086

Workings

1 *Turnover*

	£'000
Sales	5,391
Less returns inwards	39
	5,352

2 *Cost of sales*

	£'000
Opening stock	298
Purchases	2,988
Carriage inwards	20
Less returns outwards	(31)
	3,275
Less closing stock	365
	2,910

3 *Fixed assets*

	Cost £'000	Acc. depn. £'000	NBV £'000
Land	431	–	431
Buildings	512	184	328
Fixtures and fittings	389	181	208
Motor vehicles	341	204	137
Office equipment	105	56	49
	1,778	625	1,153

4 *Debtors*

	£'000
Trade debtors	619
Less provision	27
	592
Prepayments	21
	613

5 *Creditors: amounts due within one year*

	£'000
Trade creditors	331
Bank overdraft	157
Accruals (41 + 15 + 19)	75
Dividends payable	30
Corporation tax payable	211
	804

(c)   MEMO

To:	The directors
	Dowango Ltd
From:	AAT Student
Date:	30 April 20X6
Subject:	Accounts of Dowango Ltd

(i)   (1)   It is certainly possible to show the land and buildings at valuation rather than cost. Although the Companies Act 1985 states that the normal basis for the preparation of financial statements should be historical cost principles, under the alternative accounting rules, assets may be revalued.

(2)   Under the alternative accounting rules the land would be shown at its valuation of £641,000 and the buildings at their valuation of £558,000. The difference between the net book value of the assets and their new valuation would be credited to a revaluation reserve, which is an undistributable reserve. The amounts to be credited to the revaluation reserve can be calculated as follows.

	Land £'000	Buildings £'000
Valuation	641	558
NBV	431	328
	210	230

(3)   Gearing is a measure of how much long-term finance is in the form of long-term debt. If may be calculated as:

$$\frac{\text{Loan capital}}{\text{Total capital}}$$

Under the historical cost convention, total capital is £1,386,000. The gearing ratio may thus be calculated as:

$$\frac{300}{1,386} = 22\%$$

If the assets were revalued, the denominator of this ratio, ie total capital would increase by the amount credited to the revaluation reserve (£210,000 + 230,000 = £440,000). The gearing ratio would thus reduce to:

$$\frac{300}{1,826} = 16\%$$

It is possible that the lower gearing ratio may influence the bank's decision to lend the company the money to finance the acquisition. A lower gearing ratio means that the company is less risky from the bank's point of view. However, this may not be as significant when, as here, the company already has a low gearing ratio.

(4)   In future years there will be an effect on the profit and loss account. Depreciation would be calculated on the revalued amount, which is greater than historical cost. Thus the depreciation charge will be higher.

(ii)   Because the investment is a current asset – it was purchased with a view to resale – it must be valued at the lower of purchase price and net realisable value. This is in accordance with the prudence concept, which states that profits should not be anticipated but that foreseeable losses should be provided for. As we can foresee a loss on the sale of the investment, it should be shown at its realisable value of £56,000.

(iii)   The rule for valuation of stock follows the prudence concept. It is set out in SSAP *9 Stocks and long-term contracts*, which states that stock should be valued at the lower of cost and net realisable value. Furthermore, the comparison of cost and net realisable value should be done on an item by item basis, not on the total of all stocks, although similar items may be grouped together. Applying this policy would lead us to value the undervalued items at a cost of £340,000 and the overvalued items at the sales price of £15,000. The effect of this is to reduce the overall value of stock from £365,000 to £355,000 with the consequent effect of a £10,000 reduction in profit and assets.

(d) The ratios may be calculated as follows.

	Company A	Company B
Return on capital employed	$\dfrac{200}{600+400} = 20\%$	$\dfrac{420}{1,700+1,100} = 15\%$
Net profit margin	$\dfrac{200}{800} = 25\%$	$\dfrac{420}{2,100} = 20\%$
Asset turnover	$\dfrac{800}{1,000} = 0.8$	$\dfrac{2,100}{2,800} = 0.75$

Other ratios which might be useful include the following. (Note that you were asked for only *one* of these ratios.)

	Company A	Company B
Gross profit margin	$\dfrac{360}{800} = 45\%$	$\dfrac{1,050}{2,100} = 50\%$
Expenses: sales	$\dfrac{160}{800} = 20\%$	$\dfrac{630}{2,100} = 30\%$

Most of the profitability ratios indicate that Company A would be the better one to target. Return on capital employed, net profit margin and asset turnover are all higher for Company A. However, if gross profit margin is calculated, the reverse is true, and Company B appears more profitable. This suggests that it is overheads rather than underlying profitability where Company B falls short, as is confirmed when one calculates the expenses to sales ratio. The question of which company to target is therefore not clear cut. If Company B were taken over and if a more efficient management were able to keep costs down, it might prove to be the more profitable in the long run.

(e) If Dowango Ltd purchase the whole of a company's share capital, the latter company will become its subsidiary (assuming that Dowango Ltd has more than 50% of the voting rights.) Under FRS 2 *Accounting for subsidiary undertakings*, consolidated accounts would be required in addition to the accounts for the individual companies.

16 Primavera Fashions

Tutorial note. This is the *company* balance sheet. Do not worry about any consolidation aspects!

(a)   PRIMAVERA FASHIONS LIMITED
       CORRECTED BALANCE SHEET AS AT 31 MARCH 20X7

	£'000	£'000
Fixed assets		
Intangible assets		128
Tangible assets (W1)		3,273
Investments		2,924
		6,325
Current assets		
Stocks	1,178	
Debtors (W2)	833	
Cash at bank and in hand	152	
	2,163	
Creditors: amounts falling due within one year (W3)	1,209	
Net current assets		954
Total assets less current liabilities		7,279
Creditors: amounts falling due after more than one year		(1,500)
		5,779
Capital and reserves		
Called up share capital		1,000
Share premium		800
Revaluation reserve		550
Profit and loss account (W4)		3,429
		5,779

Workings

1   *Fixed assets*

	Cost	Acc depn	NBV
	£'000	£'000	£'000
Land	525	–	525
Buildings	1,000	220	780
Fixtures & fittings	1,170	346	824
Motor vehicles	1,520	583	937
Office equipment	350	143	207
	4,565	1,292	3,273

Note. The previous accountant deducted the depreciation for the year, rather than the accumulated depreciation.

2   *Debtors*

	£'000
Trade debtors	857
Less provision for doubtful debts	(61)
Plus prepayments	37
	833

3   *Creditors: amounts falling due within one year*

	£'000
Trade creditors	483
Accounts	104
Corporation tax payable	382
Dividends payable	240
	1,209

4   *Profit and loss account*

	£'000
Profit for the year per ETB	1,232
Less final dividend	240
Less corporation tax charge	382
	610
Add profit and loss a/c at 1/6/96	2,819
Profit and loss a/c at 31 March 20X7	3,429

(b)   (i)   (1)   A share premium arises when a company sells shares for a price which is higher than the nominal value. By 'premium' is meant the difference between the issue price of the share and its nominal value. For example, the shares of Primavera Fashions Ltd could have been issued at a premium of 20p per share. The accounting entries would be:

		£'000	£'000
DEBIT	Cash	1,800	
CREDIT	Share capital (4,000,000 × 25p)		1,000
CREDIT	Share premium (4,000,000 × 20p)		800

(2)   The share premium account is a statutory reserve. It is not available for the distribution of dividends.

(3)   Possible uses of the share premium account include (any one of) the following.

- Issuing bonus shares
- Writing off preliminary expenses
- Expenses of issuing shares or debentures

(ii)   The fact that the debtor went into liquidation after the end of the financial year will have an impact on the financial statements. Under SSAP 17 *Accounting for post balance sheet events*, this would be classified as an adjusting post-balance sheet event. Adjusting post balance sheet events are defined by SSAP 17 as 'post balance sheet events which provide additional evidence of conditions existing at the balance sheet date'.

The value of debtors in the balance sheet will be reduced by £24,000 and there will be a charge of £24,000 for bad debts in the profit and loss account.

(iii)   (1)   Spring Ltd is an associated company. The amount shown on the group balance sheet is therefore:

	£'000
Group share of net assets as at 31.3.X7	350
Premium paid on acquisition (W)	120
	470

Working: premium on acquisition

	£'000
Cost of investment	400
Group share of net assets (35% × 800,000)	280
Premium	120

Alternatively, the amount may be calculated as follows.

	£'000
Cost	400
Share of post-acquisition retained profits (35% £200,000)	70
	470

Only the *total* (£470,000) needs to appear in the consolidated balance sheet under the heading 'Investment in associated company'.

(2) On the notes, the investment in Spring Ltd will be analysed as follows.

	£'000
Share of net assets	350
Premium paid on acquisition	120
	470

17 Solu

Tutorial note. Make sure you know how to deal with revaluations on consolidation. This is particularly important for the minority interest in Part (d).

(a) The journal entries required are as follows.

	Debit £'000	Credit £'000
Dividends (p&l) (£400,000 × 4 × (0.06 − 0.02))	64	
Dividends payable		64
Corporation tax (p&l)	75	
Corporation tax (creditor)		75
Interest charge (p&l) (10% × £200,000 × 6/12)	10	
Accruals		10
Bad debt expense (W)	9	
Provision for bad debts		9

Working: Bad debt expense

Debtors per ETB	£500,000
Provision required (£500,000 × 2%)	£10,000
∴ Increase in provision (10 – 1)	£9,000

(b) SOLU LIMITED
PROFIT AND LOSS ACCOUNT FOR THE YEAR ENDED 31 MARCH 20X8

	£'000
Turnover (continuing operations)	4,090
Cost of sales (W1)	1,805
Gross profit	2,285
Distribution costs	1,055
Administrative expenses (W2)	999
Operating profit (continuing operations)	231
Interest payable and similar charges (W3)	20
Profit on ordinary activities before taxation	211
Tax on profit on ordinary activities	75
Profit on ordinary activities after taxation	136
Dividends (32+64)	96
Retained profit for the financial year	40

Workings

1   *Cost of sales*

	£'000
Opening stock	300
Purchases	1,800
Carriage inwards	25
Closing stock	(320)
	1,805

2   *Administrative expenses*

	£'000
Per ETB	990
Increase in bad debt prov'n	9
	999

3   *Interest payable*

	£'000
Per ETB	10
Accrual	10
	20

(c) NOTES TO THE DIRECTORS

(i)   *Land at valuation*

The Companies Act 1985 permits fixed assets to be shown at valuation rather than cost, as does the new accounting standard, FRS 15 *Tangible fixed assets*. The increase is calculated as follows.

	£'000
NBV per ETB (268 – 50)	218
Valuation	550
Increase in value	332

The entries required to adjust the accounts are as follows.

DEBIT	Land and buildings	£332,000	
CREDIT	Revaluation reserve		£332,000

Depreciation must be charged on the revalued amount.

(ii) *Accruals concept*

Under FRS 18 *Accounting policies,* revenue and costs are *accrued.* This means that they are recognised as they are earned or incurred, not as money is received or paid. They are matched with one another and dealt with in the profit and loss account of the period to which they relate.

A clear example from the accounts of Solu which illustrates the accruals concept is the accrual for six months' interest on the long-term loan. While no money has been paid out, this charge has been incurred in the last six months of 20X8 and must therefore be matched against the profits of that year.

(iii) *Subsidiary undertaking*

A company (S) is a subsidiary of its parent (P) in the following circumstances.

(1) P holds a majority of the voting rights in S.

(2) P is a member of S and had the right to appoint or remove directors holding a majority of the voting rights at meetings of the board.

(3) P has a right to exercise a dominant influence over S by virtue of the memorandum or articles or a control contract.

(4) P is a member of S and controls alone, or under an agreement with other shareholders or members, a majority of the voting rights in S.

(5) P has a participating interest in S and actually exercises a dominant influence over S or is managed on a unified basis with S.

(6) S is a subsidiary of a subsidiary of P.

(d) *Minority interest in the Solu Group as at 31 March 20X8*

	£'000	
Share capital	100	
Share premium	50	
Profit and loss account	25	
Revaluation reserve (W)	25	
	200	× 25% = £50,000

Working: revaluation reserve

	£'000
Valuation at 31.3.X8	95
NBV	70
Revaluation reserve	25

18 Bathlea

Tutorial note. In Part (c) your answer should be in terms of FRS 12 *Provisions, contingent liabilities and contingent assets*.

(a) The journal entries required are as follows.

	Debit	Credit
	£'000	£'000
Dividends (p&l) (£500,000 × 5.5)	27.5	
Dividends payable		27.5
Corporation tax (p&l)	11.0	
Corporation tax (creditor)		11.0
Interest charge (p&l) (12% × £100,000 × 1/12)	1.0	
Accruals		1.0
Bad debt expense	10.0	
Debtors		10.0
Bad debt expense (W)	5.8	
Provision for bad debts		5.8

Working: Increase in bad debt provision

	£'000
Debtors per ETB	370
Less bad debt written off	10
Adjusted debtors at 30.9.X8	360
Provision required (3% × 360)	10.8
Existing provision	5.0
∴ Increase in provision	5.8

(b)   BATHLEA LIMITED
      PROFIT AND LOSS ACCOUNT FOR THE YEAR ENDED 31 SEPTEMBER 20X8

	£'000
Turnover (continuing operations)	3,509.0
Cost of sales (W1)	1,641.0
Gross profit	1868.0
Distribution costs	857.0
Administrative expenses (W2)	907.8
Operating profit (continuing operations)	103.2
Interest payable and similar charges (11+1)	12.0
Profit on ordinary activities before taxation	91.2
Tax on profit on ordinary activities	11.0
Profit on ordinary activities after taxation	80.2
Dividends (15+27.5)	42.5
Retained profit for the financial year	37.7

BATHLEA LIMITED
BALANCE SHEET AS AT 31 SEPTEMBER 20X8

	£'000	£'000
Fixed assets		
Tangible assets (W3)		500.0
Current assets		
Stocks	250.0	
Debtors (W4)	359.2	
	609.2	
Creditors: amounts falling due within one year (W5)	401.5	
		207.7
Total assets less current liabilities		707.7
Creditors: amounts falling due after more than one year		100.0
		607.7
Capital and reserves		
Called up share capital		500.0
Profit and loss account (W6)		107.7
		607.7

Workings

1   *Cost of sales*

	£'000
Opening stock	200
Purchases	1,600
Carriage inwards	91
Closing stock	(250)
	1,641

2 *Administrative expenses*

	£'000
Per ETB	892.0
Bad debt written off	10.0
Increase in bad debt provision	5.8
	907.8

3 *Fixed assets*

	Cost £'000	Acc. depn. £'000	NBV £'000
Land and buildings	300	65	235
Fixtures and fittings	220	43	177
Motor vehicles	70	27	43
Office equipment	80	35	45
	670	170	500

4 *Debtors*

	£'000
Per ETB	370.0
Bad debt written off	(10.0)
Bad debt provision	(10.8)
Prepayment	10.0
	359.2

5 *Creditors: amounts falling due within one year*

	£'000
Per ETB	350.0
Accruals (9 + 1)	10.0
Taxation	11.0
Dividends	27.5
Bank overdraft	3.0
	401.5

6 *Profit and loss account*

	£'000
Profit and loss account b/f	70.0
Profit for the year	37.7
Profit and loss account c/f	107.7

(c)   NOTES FOR DIRECTORS ON ACCOUNTING STANDARDS

(i) *Law suit*

The law suit is a contingent liability and, as such is governed by FRS 12 *Provisions, contingent liabilities and contingent assets*. FRS 12 defines a contingent liability as:

'A possible obligation that arises from past events and whose existence will be confirmed only by the occurrence or non-occurrence of one or more uncertain future events not wholly within the entity's control'.

Under FRS 12, a contingent liability should never be accrued for in the accounts – if the outflow is probable, the item is a provision. If the outflow is merely possible, a contingent liability should be disclosed. However, in this case the possibility of an outflow is remote so there is no need to disclose or provide.

(ii) *Development expenditure*

The treatment of development expenditure is governed by SSAP 13 *Accounting for research and development*. The standard states that development expenditure is incurred with a particular commercial aim in view and in the reasonable expectation of earning profits or reducing costs. It is therefore appropriate that in these circumstances development costs should be deferred (capitalised) and matched against the future revenues.

Development costs may, however, only be capitalised when certain strict criteria are met.

(1) There is a clearly defined project.
(2) The related expenditure is separately identifiable.
(2) The project is technically feasible and commercially viable.
(3) All further costs will be more than covered by related future revenues.
(4) The company has adequate resources to complete the project.

Where development expenditure is capitalised, its amortisation should begin with the commercial production of the product, and should be written off over the period in which the product is expected to be sold.

19 Mattesich

MATTESICH LIMITED
PROFIT AND LOSS ACCOUNT FOR THE YEAR ENDED 30 SEPTEMBER 20X0

	£'000	£'000
Turnover		
Continuing operations (W1)	36,521	
Acquisitions	2,714	
	39,235	
Discontinued operations	1,213	
		40,448
Cost of sales (W2)		18,173
Gross profit		22,275
Distribution costs		5,863
Administrative expenses		3,469
Operating profit		
Continuing operations (W3)	12,327	
Acquisitions	603	
	12,930	
Discontinued operations	13	
		12,943
Loss on disposal of discontinued operations		473
		12,470
Interest payable		544
Profit on ordinary activities before taxation		11,926
Tax on profit on ordinary activities		3,813
Profit on ordinary activities after taxation		8,113
Dividends (W4)		4,900
Retained profit for the financial year		3,213

Workings

1   *Turnover – continuing operations*

	£'000	£'000
Sales per ETB		40,448
Less: acquisitions	2,714	
discontinued operations	1,213	
		(3,927)
		36,521

2   *Cost of sales*

	£'000
Opening stock	12,973
Purchases	18,682
	31,655
Closing stock	(13,482)
	18,173

3   *Operating profit – continuing operations*

	£'000
Gross profit	22,275
Distribution costs	5,863
Administrative expenses	3,469
Operating profit	12,943
Less: acquisitions	603
discontinued operations	13
	12,327

4   *Dividends*

	£'000
Interim: 14,000,000 × 15p	2,100
Final: 14,000,000 × 20p	2,800
	4,900

20 Brecked

(a)

		£'000	£'000
DEBIT	Dividend (profit and loss) (3,000 × 10p)	300	
CREDIT	Dividend payable		300
DEBIT	Stock (balance sheet)	5,346	
CREDIT	Stock (P&L)		5,346
DEBIT	Taxation (P&L)	1,473	
CREDIT	Taxation payable		1,473
DEBIT	Depreciation charge	1,115	
CREDIT	Accumulated depreciation		
	Buildings		65
	Fixtures and fittings		217
	Motor vehicles		648
	Office equipment		185
DEBIT	Land (6,000 – 5,150)	850	
CREDIT	Revaluation reserve		850
DEBIT	Damages	250	
CREDIT	Provision for damages		250

(b)

	Land £'000	Buildings £'000	Fixtures & fittings £'000	Motor vehicles £'000	Office equipment £'000	Total £'000
Cost valuation						
1 April 20X0	5,150	3,073	2,169	4,244	659	15,295
Additions	–	–	–	1,340	268	1,608
Revaluation	850	–	–	–	–	850
Disposals	–	–	–	(975)	–	(975)
31 March 20X1	6,000	3,073	2,169	4,609	927	16,778
Accumulated depreciation						
1 April 20X0		420	756	2,520	382	4,078
Charge for year		65	217	648	185	1,115
Disposals		–	–	(506)	–	(506)
31 March 20X1		485	973	2,662	567	4,687
Net book value						
31 March 20X1	6,000	2,588	1,196	1,947	360	12,091
31 March 20X0	5,150	2,653	1,413	1,724	277	11,217

(c)   The treatment of the damages claim is governed by FRS 12 *Provisions, contingent liabilities and contingent assets.* FRS 12 details the circumstances in which provisions should be recognised.

(i)   An entity has a **present obligation** (legal or constructive) as a result of a past event.

(ii)   It is probable that a **transfer of economic benefits** will be required to settle the obligation.

(iii)   A **reliable estimate** can be made of the obligation.

In the case of the damages claim there is a present obligation (a) to pay damages. The lawyer has stated that this transfer of economic benefits is probable (b). In addition the amount of the claim has been estimated reliably (c) at £250,000, so a provision for this amount should be set up in the accounts.

21 Leger

(a)   LEGER LIMITED
      PROFIT AND LOSS ACCOUNT FOR THE YEAR ENDED 30 SEPTEMBER 20X1

	£'000	£'000
Turnover		
Continuing operations	21,324	
		21,324
Cost of sales (W1)		9,383
Gross profit		11,941
Distribution costs		3,415
Administrative expenses		2,607
Operating profit		
Continuing operations	5,919	
Profit on ordinary activities before interest		5,919
Interest payable (W2)		360
Profit on ordinary activities		
before taxation		5,559
Tax on profit on ordinary activities		1,567
Profit on ordinary activities after taxation		3,992
Dividends (W3)		675
Retained profit for the financial year		3,317

Workings

1   *Cost of sales*

	£'000
Opening stock	3,127
Purchases	11,581
Carriage inwards	83
	14,791
Less closing stock	5,408
	9,383

2   *Interest payable*

	£'000
Per trial balance	180
Plus accrual 4,000 × 9% × 6/12	180
	360

3   *Dividends*

	£'000
Interim	300
Final: 2,500 × 15p	375
	675

(b)   LEGER LIMITED
        NOTE OF HISTORICAL COST PROFITS AND LOSSES
        FOR THE YEAR ENDED 30 SEPTEMBER 20X1

	£'000
Reported profit on ordinary activities before taxation	5,559
Difference between historical cost depreciation and the actual depreciation charge of the year calculated on the revalued amount (72 – 62)	10
Historical cost profit on ordinary activities before taxation	5,569
Historical cost retained profit (3,317 + 10)	3,327

22 Typeset

Tutorial note. Remember to take into account the adjustments to the retained profit given in the ETB. Investments could also be shown under current assets.

TYPESET LIMITED
BALANCE SHEET AS AT 31 MARCH 20X9

	£'000	£'000
Fixed assets		
Tangible assets (W1)		5,820
Investments		1,580
		7,400
Current assets		
Stocks	4,187	
Debtors (W2)	3,153	
Cash at bank and in hand	216	
	7,556	
Creditors: amounts falling due within one year (W4)	2,728	
Net current assets		4,828
Total assets less current liabilities		12,228
Creditors: amounts falling due after one year		
Long-term loan		1,450
		10,778
Capital and reserves		
Called up share capital		5,000
Share premium		1,200
Revaluation reserve		500
Profit and loss account (W5)		4,078
		10,778

Workings

1   *Tangible assets*

	Cost	Acc. Depn.	NBV
	£'000	£'000	£'000
Land	2,075	-	2,075
Buildings	2,077	383	1,694
Fixtures and fittings	1,058	495	563
Motor vehicles	2,344	1,237	1,107
Office equipment	533	152	381
	8,087	2,267	5,820

2   *Debtors*

	£'000
Trade debtors per trial balance	3,136
Less provision for doubtful debts (W3)	80
	3,056
Prepayments	97
	3,153

3   *Provision for doubtful debts*

	£'000
Debtors per trial balance	3,136
Less doubtful debt	36
	3,100
Provision for doubtful debt:	
3,100 × 2%	62
Add 50% of doubtful debt	18
Total provision	80
Existing provision	37
∴ Increase in provision	43

4   *Creditors: amounts falling due within one year*

	£'000
Trade creditors	1,763
Corporation tax payable	493
Dividends payable	350
Accruals	122
	2,728

5   *Profit and loss account*

	£'000
At 1 April 20X8	3,533
Retained profit for the year (W6)	545
At 31 March 20X9	4,078

6   *Retained profit for the year*

	£'000
Retained profit per trial balance	1,431
Dividend payable	(350)
Corporation tax	(493)
Increase in doubtful debt provision	(43)
	545

Chapter 10 cash flow statements

23 Paton

PATON LIMITED
RECONCILIATION OF OPERATING PROFIT
TO NET CASH INFLOW FROM OPERATING ACTIVITIES
FOR THE YEAR ENDED 30 SEPTEMBER 20X1

	£'000
Operating profits	5,938
Add depreciation charge	2,007
Less profit on sale of fixed asset	(131)
Increase in stock (7,420 – 6,823)	(597)
Increase in debtors (4,122 – 3,902)	(220)
Increase in creditors (1,855 – 1,432)	423
Net cash inflow from operating activities	7,420

24 Fun and games

(a)   GAMES LIMITED
RECONCILIATION OF OPERATING PROFIT
TO NET CASH INFLOW FROM OPERATING ACTIVITIES

	£'000
Operating profit (246 + 56)	302
Depreciation	277
Increase in stocks (918 – 873)	(45)
Increase in debtors (751 – 607)	(144)
Increase in creditors (583 – 512)	71
Net cash inflow from operating activities	461

(b)   NOTES FOR BOARD MEETING ON MINORITY INTEREST

(i)   *Calculation of minority interest*

	£'000
Share capital	1,000
Share premium	100
Profit and loss account	1,180
Revaluation reserve (W)	200
	2,480 × 25% = £620,000

Working: revaluation reserve

	£'000
Book value of fixed assets	1,845
Fair value of fixed assets	2,045
Difference to revaluation reserve	200

(ii)   *Presentation of minority interest*

The minority interest will be disclosed as part of share capital and reserves, separately after the share capital and reserves attributable to the group.

(iii)   *Definition of minority interest*

FRS 2 *Accounting for subsidiary undertakings* defines a minority interest as the interest in a subsidiary undertaking included in the consolidation that is attributable to the shares held by persons other than the parent undertaking and its subsidiaries.

25 Edlin

Tutorial note. The trickiest part of the cash flow statement, assuming you're familiar with the method, is the fixed asset working. Study our solution carefully if you slipped up. In part (c) you are asked to *comment* on the ratios as well as calculating them – make sure you do this.

(a)   EDLIN LIMITED
RECONCILIATION OF OPERATING PROFIT
TO NET CASH INFLOW FROM OPERATING ACTIVITIES

	£'000
Operating profit	650
Depreciation	175
Profit on sale of asset	(5)
Increase in stocks	(20)
Increase in debtors	(90)
Increase in creditors	40
Net cash inflow from operating activities	750

(b) EDLIN LIMITED
CASH FLOW STATEMENT FOR THE YEAR ENDED 31 MARCH 20X8

	£'000
Net cash inflow from operating activities	750
Returns on investment and servicing of finance	
Interest paid	(15)
Taxation (20X7 creditor, paid y/e 31.3.X8)	(35)
Capital expenditure and financial investment (Note 1)	(522)
	178
Equity dividends paid (20X7 creditor, paid y/e 31.3.X8)	(50)
	128
Financing (Note 1)	70
Increase in cash	198

Note 1: Gross cash flows

Capital expenditure and financial investment

	£'000
Proceeds of sale of fixed asset (W)	13
Purchase of fixed assets	(535)
	(522)

Financing

Issue of shares	£'000
Share capital	20
Share premium	20
	40
Increase in loan (150 – 120)	30
	70

Working: proceeds of sale of fixed asset

	£'000
Net book value: 20 – (20 × 3/5)	8
Profit	5
∴ Proceeds	13

(c) *Gearing ratio*

	20X8	20X7
$\dfrac{\text{Long-term loan}}{\text{Long-term loan plus capital and reserves}}$	$\dfrac{150}{150+740}=17\%$	$\dfrac{120}{120+265}=31\%$

OR:

	20X8	20X7
$\dfrac{\text{Long-term loan}}{\text{Capital and reserves}}$	$\dfrac{150}{740}=20\%$	$\dfrac{120}{265}=45\%$

	20X8	20X7
Current ratio		
$\dfrac{\text{Current assets}}{\text{Current liabilities}}$	$\dfrac{688}{350} = 2.0$	$\dfrac{380}{195} = 1.9$

Comments

The gearing ratio, whichever way it is calculated has decreased significantly in 20X8. This is because, although the loan has increased, this has been more than offset by an increase in share capital and reserves. Since a high-geared company can be a more risky investment, it is comforting to know that Edlin Ltd is financing its expansion from a variety of sources other than debt.

The current ratio is more or less unchanged. Again this is a good sign. The company is expanding, and this can sometimes lead to overtrading. Edlin Ltd clearly has this under control.

26 Angle

ANGLE LIMITED
CASH FLOW STATEMENT FOR THE YEAR ENDED 31 MARCH 20X1

	£'000	£'000
Net cash inflow from operating activities		2,376
Returns on investments and servicing of finance		
Interest paid		(202)
Taxation		(370)
Capital expenditure		
Payment to acquire tangible fixed assets (W)		(3,653)
		(1,849)
Equity dividends paid		(400)
Net cash outflow before financing		(2,249)
Financing		
Increase in long term loan	1,000	
Issue of share capital (3,000 – 2,200)	800	
Share premium (1,200 – 400)	800	
		2,600
Increase in cash		351

Working: payments to acquire tangible fixed assets

FIXED ASSETS

	£'000		£'000
Balance b/d	4,009	Depreciation	875
Revaluation	500		
Additions (bal fig)	3,653	Balance c/d	7,287
	8,162		8,162

27 Roth

Notes to explain fall in cash balance in 20X1

From the information given, it can be deduced that the cash balance has fallen considerably from £1,843,000 in 20X0 to £234,000 in 20X1.

Looking at the reconciliation from operating profit to net cash inflow from operating activities, it can be seen that **operating profit is healthy**. However, there has been an **increase in debtors** of £3,584,000, despite sales being described as similar in each of the two years. This needs to be investigated – it suggest **debtors are paying more slowly** or there is a problem with bad debts. Tighter credit control needs to be enforced.

Cash flow has also been adversely affected by the fact that the company is **paying its creditors more quickly**. This can be seen from the decrease in creditors of £1,031,000. The combined impact of faster creditor payment and slower debtor collection is £4,615,000, accounting for most of the decrease in cash inflow from operating activities.

The next two items on the cash flow statement, **interest and tax are unavoidable costs** to the company, although the increase in the loan may account for the higher interest payments.

Turning to the capital expenditure heading, we see that the company has **invested quite heavily in fixed** assets, and the financing section tells us that this has been paid for mainly by increasing or taking out a loan. While fixed assets are intended to generate cash flows in the future, the short-term impact on the cash balance is unfavourable.

The **dividends** paid amounted to £5,000,000. This figure is **very high** considering the profit is £8,763,000, and has clearly been funded by depleting the cash reserves. The actual cash available to pay dividends was the operating cash flow of £5,959,000 less interest of £542,000 and tax of £2,017,000, that is £3,400,000. Unless the debtor collection situation improves next year, the company may have to **reconsider its dividend policy**, in which cash, as well as profit, should play a part. It is, however, possible that sales may increase to fund a similar level of dividend payment, but it would be a good idea to address the credit control issues in any case.

Chapter 11 Ratio analysis

28 Magnus Carter

REPORT

To: Magnus Carter
From: A Technician
Date: 23 June 20X1

Performance of Baron Ltd

The purpose of this report is to help you to interpret the financial statements of Baron Ltd. This will be done using certain key ratios, the meaning of which will be explained. In addition, the report will identify areas that could be improved over the next year.

(a)   *Calculation of the ratios*

	20X1	*20X0*

Gross profit percentage

$$\frac{\text{Gross profit}}{\text{Turnover}} \qquad \frac{1,204}{1,852} = 65\% \qquad \frac{1,116}{1,691} = 66\%$$

Net profit percentage

$$\frac{\text{PBT}}{\text{Turnover}} \qquad \frac{519}{1,852} = 28\% \qquad \frac{592}{1,691} = 35\%$$

Debtor turnover in days

$$\frac{\text{Debtors}}{\text{Sales per day}} \qquad \frac{319}{1,852} \times 365 = 63 \text{ days} \qquad \frac{236}{1,691} \times 361 = 51 \text{ days}$$

Creditor turnover in days

$$\frac{\text{Creditors}}{\text{Cost of sales per day}} \qquad \frac{48}{648} \times 365 = 27 \text{ days} \qquad \frac{44}{575} \times 365 = 28 \text{ days}$$

Stock turnover in days

$$\frac{\text{Stock}}{\text{Cost of sales}} \times 365 \qquad \frac{217}{648} \times 365 = 122 \text{ days} \qquad \frac{159}{575} \times 365 = 101 \text{ days}$$

(b)   **Explanation and comment**

(i)   **Gross profit percentage**

This ratio shows the percentage of gross profit generated by the company's sales, and is thus an indication of the gross profit margin on sales.

The gross profit percentage of Baron Ltd has decreased, but only very slightly, from 66% to 65%. However, in absolute terms, turnover and profit have increased. It is clear that the company has not had to resort to lower margins in order to increase sales.

(ii)   **Net profit percentage**

As the name suggests, this shows the percentage of net profit generated by the company's sales. Net profit takes account of expenses as well as cost of sales.

The net profit percentage of Baron Ltd has gone down from 35% to 28%. As the gross profit margin has remained stable, the decline must be due to a higher percentage of expenses to sales. In absolute terms, the actual net profit is down from £592,000 to £519,000, so it is clear that expenses are a problem.

(iii) **Debtors turnover**

This ratio is a rough measure of the average length of time it takes for a company's debtors to pay what they owe. This measure is only approximate, because the balance sheet value of debtors may be abnormally high or low compared with the normal level the company usually has.

The ratio has got worse – it takes the company around 12 more days to collect debts in 20X1 compared with 20X0. There could be a number of reasons for this. Perhaps the company has been selling to less reliable credit customers in a drive to increase sales, or perhaps it is a question of poor credit control.

(iv) **Creditors turnover**

This ratio shows the average number of days it takes the company to pay its creditors. It is a measure of a company's liquidity; an increase in creditor days is often a sign of lack of long-term finance or poor management of current assets, resulting in the use of extended credit from suppliers.

Baron Ltd's credit turnover has remained about the same, showing that this is not a problem for the company.

(v) **Stock turnover**

This figure indicates the average number of days that items of stock are held for, or, from another point of view, how quickly the stock is selling.

Baron Ltd's stock turnover has increased from 101 days to 122 days. This is a matter of concern, as it is not a good idea for too much working capital to be tied up in stock. Possibly some of the stock is obsolete and may need writing down or off.

(c) **Areas for improvement**

From the ratios calculated above it is clear that there are a number of areas of concern. The company is **expanding**, showing growth in turnover and gross profit, but it is important that this is not at the expense of control of debtors, stock and expenses.

A **review of debt collection** procedures needs to be carried out and potential defaulting debtors identified. Some debtors may simply need chasing up; others may pose more of a risk and the company should reconsider whether it is appropriate to offer credit to such customers.

A review also needs to be carried out of **stock control procedures, paying** particular attention to identifying any obsolete stock.

Finally, thought must be given to the **control of expenses** – there is no point in expanding if the profit is going to be swallowed up in overheads.

29 Bins

REPORT

To:	The Directors, Binns Ltd
From:	A Technician
Date:	17 January 20X8
Subject:	Financial statements of Gone Ltd

Introduction

The report analyses the financial statements of Gone Ltd with a view to assessing its suitability as a supplier for our company. The report shows certain key ratios covering profitability, liquidity and gearing. A comparison is made between 20X7 and 20X6 and also with the industry average for the year.

Summary of ratios

The ratios are summarised below. Calculations are shown in an appendix to this report.

	20X7	20X6
Return on capital employed	5.6%	11.1%
Gross profit percentage	39%	45%
Net profit percentage	11%	20.8%
Current ratio	1.2:1	2.1:1
Gearing	42.5%	20.5%

Profitability

Net profitability has declined in 20X7 in absolute terms as compared with 20X6 from £270,000 to £198,000, although gross profit has risen from £585,000 to £702,000. This is due to increased expenses – perhaps costs are not being kept under control. Turnover has increased. Possible an advertising campaign has been needed to expand the company's product range, although more information would be required to determine whether this is the case.

As regards profitability ratios, the 20X7 results show a decline as compared with 20X6. Return on capital employed and net profit margin are particularly worrying, having fallen by 50%. The 20X7 ratios for gross profit margin, net profit margin and return on capital employed are all below the industry average. In 20X6 the gross profit margin was above average, but this has now declined.

Overall the profitability figures are not particularly impressive. It is possible that some of this is due to the company's recent expansion – it has invested in fixed assets which have increased turnover but not profits as yet.

Liquidity

The current ratio is significantly worse in 20X7 than in 20X6 – 1.2 as opposed to 2.1. It is also much less in 20X7 than the industry average, whereas in 20X6 it was higher. This is a cause for concern, although the information does not show the components of current assets. If the fall is due to reduced stock levels, this is less of a worry than a lower bank balance.

Gearing

As we are considering Gone Ltd as a potential supplier, we should be very wary of any factors which suggest that it may not be able to continue in business. High gearing is one such factor. Large debts carry risk of insolvency, and the company may have difficulty meeting interest payments.

The level of gearing has doubled in 20X7 and has gone from being comfortably below the industry average to worryingly above it. This, more than profitability or liquidity should be of concern to us. The company has used debt finance rather than equity to expand its fixed asset base, but has not as yet increased profits.

Conclusion

On the basis of the above analysis, particularly as regards the level of gearing, I would recommend that we use an alternative supplier. It is possible that Gone Ltd's investment in fixed assets will lead to a successful expansion of the business in the future, in which case we should reconsider our decision.

APPENDIX: CALCULATION OF RATIOS

	20X7	20X6
Return on capital employed	$\dfrac{198}{2,034 + 1,506} = 5.6\%$	$\dfrac{270}{1,938 + 500} = 11.1\%$
Gross profit percentage	$\dfrac{702}{1,800} = 39\%$	$\dfrac{585}{1,300} = 45\%$
Net profit percentage	$\dfrac{198}{1,800} = 11\%$	$\dfrac{270}{1,300} = 20.8\%$
Current ratio	$\dfrac{460}{383} = 1.2{:}1$	$\dfrac{853}{406} = 2.1{:}1$
Gearing	$\dfrac{1,506}{2,034 + 1,506} = 42.5\%$	$\dfrac{500}{1,938 + 500} = 20.5\%$

30 Byrne and May

REPORT

To: Duncan Tweedy
From: A Technician
Date: 23 October 20X0
Relative Profitability of Byrne Ltd and May Ltd

The purpose of this report is to help you to assess the relative profitability of Byrne Ltd and May Ltd. This will be done using certain key ratios, the meaning of which will be explained. Other information provided in the financial statements of the two companies will also be taken into account.

(a) **Return on capital employed**

This ratio shows in percentage terms how much profit is being generated by the capital employed in the company. May Ltd shows a higher return on capital employed, and is therefore more profitable per £ of capital employed in the business. However, it should be noted that in absolute terms, Byrne Ltd is making more profit; it is just not using its capital as effectively.

(b) **Gross profit percentage**

This ratio shows the percentage of gross profit generated by the company's sales, and is thus an indication of the gross profit margin on sales.

The gross profit percentage of May Ltd is higher than that of Byrne Ltd, indicating that it is selling at higher margins. Byrne Ltd's higher turnover may be at the expense of lower margins.

(c) **Net profit percentage**

As the name suggests, this shows the percentage of net profit generated by the company's sales. Net profit takes account of expenses as well as cost of sales.

The net profit percentage of May Ltd is also higher than that of Byrne Ltd. Part of the difference is accounted for by the fact that the gross profit percentage is higher, but it also indicates that May Ltd is controlling its expenses more effectively.

(d) **Earnings per share**

This is a measure of the return to shareholders in the year and shows in pence the profit after tax earned for each ordinary share.

May Ltd's earnings per share is considerably higher than that of Byrne Ltd, showing that shareholders are getting more out of their investment.

Conclusion

May Ltd is the more profitable, in terms of all four key ratios. Although the Byrne is the larger company in terms of turnover, profit and asset base, it is clear that May Ltd is making better use of those assets and giving a better return to shareholders.

31 Animalets

(a) REPORT

To: The Directors, Animalets plc
From: A Technician
Date: 20 November 20X8

Performance and position of Superpet Ltd

As requested, I have analysed the performance and position of Superpet Ltd with special reference to selected accounting ratios. The calculation of the ratios is shown in the Appendix attached to this report.

General

Superpet is clearly expanding; both turnover and profit are up on 20X7. The company has invested in new fixed assets by increasing borrowing and issuing share capital.

Gross profit ratio

This has increased slightly from 53% in 20X7 to 58% in 20X8. This is due to a large increase in turnover and the fact that the cost of sales has not increased in proportion to the sales. Clearly, then, the company is not achieving increased sales at the expense of lower margins.

Current ratio

The current ratio has fallen slightly, but not significantly. It is still reasonably healthy. Sometimes expansion can give rise to overtrading, but this has not happened with Superpet.

Acid test ratio

This ratio, because it excludes stock, may be regarded as a better indicator of the company's liquidity than the current ratio. Despite Superpet's expansion, the acid test ratio is healthy and shows a slight improvement on the previous year.

Gearing ratio

As mentioned above, Superpet has had to finance expansion by raising capital. Encouragingly, although the loan has increased, the gearing ratio, which was very low, has fallen. This is because there has been a proportionally greater increase in the capital and reserves.

Conclusion

Overall, Superpet Ltd is expanding and healthy and the ratios do not give any cause for concern.

APPENDIX – CALCULATION OF RATIOS

	20X8	*20X7*
Gross profit	$\dfrac{1,150}{2,000} = 58\%$	$\dfrac{800}{1,500} = 53\%$
Current ratio $\dfrac{\text{Current assets}}{\text{Current liabilities}}$	$\dfrac{870}{670} = 1.3$	$\dfrac{610}{448} = 1.4$
Acid test ratio $\dfrac{\text{Current assets less stock}}{\text{Current liabilities}}$	$\dfrac{(870-350)}{670} = 0.8$	$\dfrac{(610-300)}{448} = 0.7$
Gearing ratio $\dfrac{\text{Long - term loan}}{\text{Long - term loan} + \text{capital \& reserves}}$	$\dfrac{100}{1,338} = 7\%$	$\dfrac{70}{800} = 9\%$
or $\dfrac{\text{Long - term loan}}{\text{Capital \& reserves}}$	$\dfrac{100}{1,238} = 8\%$	$\dfrac{70}{730} = 10\%$

(b) SUPERPET LIMITED
RECONCILIATION OF OPERATING PROFIT
TO NET CASH INFLOW FROM OPERATING ACTIVITIES

	£'000
Operating profit	958
Depreciation	65
Profit on sale of asset	(5)
Increase in stocks	(50)
Increase in debtors	(150)
Increase in creditors	42
	860

32 Gint

AAT Student
ABC Accountants
Blank Road
Blank Town

24 June 20X1

Dear Ms Grieg

Performance of Gint Ltd

As requested I am writing to give you advice on the performance and financial position of Gint Ltd. You should find this advice useful in deciding whether to lend money to the company. I have based my analysis around a number of key ratios, shown in an appendix to this letter.

Current ratio

This is a liquidity ratio, showing the extent to which a company's current liabilities are covered by current assets. Generally speaking, a current ratio of less than one gives cause for concern – if a company cannot pay its creditors, it may go out of business.

Gint Ltd's current ratio is healthy and has shown an increase on the previous year. However, the cash balance has gone down, so the liquidity is not as good as it might be.

Quick ratio/acid test

The quick ratio shows how many assets, excluding stock, are available to meet the current liabilities. Stock is excluded because it is not always readily convertible into cash. The quick ratio or acid test is therefore a better indicator of a company's true liquidity than the current ratio which does not exclude stock.

Gint's ratio has declined. In 20X0 it had almost enough current assets (excluding stock) to cover its current liabilities. In 20X1, however, there is a considerable shortfall. The company would be advised to get a cash injection in order to avoid liquidity problems.

Gearing ratio

As we are considering lending money to Gint Ltd, we should be very wary of any factors which suggest that it may not be able to continue in business. High gearing is one such factor. Large debts carry risk of insolvency and the company may have difficulty meeting interest payments.

The gearing ratio can be calculated in two ways: debt/equity and debt/capital employed. Gint's ratio, whichever way it is calculated, has risen slightly compared with 20X0. However, it is still low, and therefore the company is not risky in this respect.

Interest cover

The interest cover ratio shows whether a company is earning enough profits before interest and tax to pay its interest costs comfortably or whether its interest costs are high in relation to the size of its profits. Low levels of cover may make it difficult for a company to borrow more funds.

Gint's interest cover has increased from last year and is healthy.

Conclusion

This is a growing company with healthy increase in turnover and profits. The company would not have problems meeting interest payments on a loan, and gearing is low. Liquidity ratios give some cause for concern: much of the company's working capital is tied up in stock, rather than more liquid assets. However, a cash injection by way of a loan would ease Gint's liquidity problems and enable it to grow. In conclusion, on the basis of my analysis, I would recommend that a loan should be made to Gint Ltd.

Yours sincerely

AAT Student

APPENDIX: CALCULATION OF RATIOS

	20X1	*20X0*
Current ratio	$\dfrac{1,663}{723} = 2.3$	$\dfrac{1,301}{650} = 2.00$
Quick ratio/acid test	$\dfrac{506}{723} = 0.7$	$\dfrac{585}{650} = 0.9$
Gearing ratio		
Debt/equity	$\dfrac{600}{4,712} = 12.7\%$	$\dfrac{500}{4,492} = 11.1\%$
Debt/capital employed	$\dfrac{600}{5,312} = 11.3\%$	$\dfrac{500}{4,992} = 10\%$
Interest cover	$\dfrac{552}{46} = 12$	$\dfrac{410}{41} = 10$

Chapter 12 Introduction to group accounts

33 Two options

(a) If Animalets were to purchase 30% of the shares of Superpet, giving the directors significant influence over Superpet, the latter would be an *associate* of Animalets. The accounting treatment would then follow FRS 9 and is known as *equity accounting*.

Consolidated profit and loss account

(i) Animalets' share of the operating profit of Superpet should be included immediately after group operating results.

(ii) From the level of profit before tax, Animalets' share of the relevant amounts of Superpet should be included within amounts for the group.

(iii) Group share of Superpet's tax should be disclosed in a note.

Consolidated balance sheet

(i) Group share of net assets of Superpet should be disclosed.

(ii) Goodwill on acquisition, less any amortisation should be disclosed separately.

(b)　If Animalets were to purchase a 75% stake, together with dominant influence, Superpet would be a *subsidiary* of Animalets. In the consolidated accounts, the income and expenditure and the assets and liabilities of Superpet would be added on a line-by-line basis to those of Animalets under *acquisition accounting.* The remaining 25% of the shares not acquired by Animalets would be shown as a minority interest.

34 MacNeal

CALCULATION OF GOODWILL ON CONSOLIDATION
ARISING ON ACQUISITION OF MACNEAL LTD

	£'000	£'000
Cost of investment		5,000
Net assets acquired		
Share capital	1,200	
Share premium	800	
Revaluation reserve (W1)	1,000	
Profit and loss account	2,800	
	5,800	
Group share (W2): 75%		4,350
		650

Workings

1　*Revaluation reserve*

	£'000
Fair value of fixed assets	5,844
Book value of fixed assets	4,844
Revaluation reserve	1,000

2　*Group share*

$$\frac{900}{1,200} \text{ shares} = 75\%$$

Chapters 13 and 14 Further aspects of group accounting

35 Norman

NORMAN LIMITED
CONSOLIDATED BALANCE SHEET AS AT 31 MARCH 20X1

	£'000	£'000
Fixed assets		
Intangible fixed asset: goodwill (460 − 46)		414
Tangible fixed assets (12,995 + 1,755 + 400)		15,150
Current assets		
Stock (3,586 + 512)	4,098	
Debtors (2,193 + 382)	2,575	
Cash (84 + 104)	188	
	6,861	
Creditors: amounts falling due within one year		
Trade creditors (1,920 + 273)	2,193	
Proposed dividend	160	
Taxation (667 + 196)	863	
	3,216	
Net current assets		3,645
Creditors: amounts falling due after more than one year		
Long-term loan		(400)
		18,809
Capital and reserves		
Called up share capital		2,000
Reserves (W5)		16,238
		18,238
Minority interests (W4)		571
		18,809

Workings

1 *Group structure*

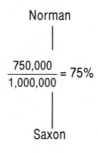

$$\frac{750{,}000}{1{,}000{,}000} = 75\%$$

Norman

Saxon

PROFESSIONAL EDUCATION

2   *Revaluation reserve: Saxon*

	£'000
Fair value of fixed assets	2,047
Book value of fixed assets	1,647
Revaluation reserve	400

3   *Goodwill*

	£'000	£'000
Cost of investment		1,978
Fair value of net assets acquired		
Share capital	1,000	
Share premium	400	
Revaluation reserve	200	
Reserves at acquisition	424	
	2,024	
Group share 75%		1,518
Goodwill		460

Amortised over 10 years at £46,000 pa

4   *Minority interests*

	£'000
Saxon's net assets per question at 31 March 20X1	1,884
Add revaluation reserve (W2)	400
	2,284

∴ Minority interests = £2,284,000 × 25% = £571,000

5   *Reserves*

	Norman	*Saxon*
	£'000	£'000
Per question	16,089	684
Less pre-acquisition		(424)
		260
Saxon: 260 × 75%	195	
Amortisation of goodwill	(46)	
	16,238	

36 Checkoff

CHECKOFF PLC
CONSOLIDATED PROFIT AND LOSS ACCOUNT
FOR THE YEAR ENDED 31 MARCH 20X1

	£'000
Turnover (W1)	20,200
Cost of sales (W2)	10,300
Gross profit	9,900
Distribution costs	2,450
Administrative expenses	2,080
Profit on ordinary activities before interest	5,370
Interest paid and similar charges	920
Profit on ordinary activities before taxation	4,450
Tax on profit on ordinary activities	1,490
Profit on ordinary activities after taxation	2,960
Minority interests (W3)	220
Profit for the financial year	2,740
Dividends	750
Retained profit for the financial year	1,990

Workings

1   *Turnover*

	£'000
Checkoff	15,800
Pooshkin	5,400
Less intercompany	(1,000)
	20,200

2   *Cost of sales*

	£'000
Checkoff	8,500
Pooshkin	2,800
Less intercompany	(1,000)
	10,300

3   *Minority interest*

Pooshkin's profit after tax = £880,000
∴ Minority interests = £880,000 × 25%
= £220,000

Answers to Full Exam based Assessments

JUNE 2002 EXAM PAPER

ANSWERS

DO NOT TURN THIS PAGE UNTIL YOU HAVE COMPLETED THE EXAM

Section 1

Part A

TASK 1.1

(a) **BPP Note.** All figures are the aggregate of the two profit and loss account or balance sheet figures unless other wise indicated.

LAWTON LIMITED
CONSOLIDATED PROFIT AND LOSS ACCOUNT
FOR THE YEAR ENDED 30 APRIL 20X3

	£'000
Turnover (W2)	4,240
Cost of sales (W2)	2,760
Gross profit	1,480
Distribution costs	340
Administration expenses	260
	880
Amortisation of goodwill: 95/5	19
Operating profit	861
Investment income (W3)	4
Profit on ordinary activities before taxation	865
Tax on profit on ordinary activities	260
Profit on ordinary activities after taxation	605
Minority interests: 180 × 25%	45
Group profit for the year	560
Proposed dividends	280
Retained profit for the year	280

(b)   LAWTON LIMITED
       CONSOLIDATED BALANCE SHEET
       AS AT 30 APRIL 20X3

	£'000	£'000
Fixed assets		
Intangible: goodwill (W4)		38
Tangible assets at net book value		1,660
		1,698
Current assets		
Stock at cost	880	
Debtors (W5)	720	
Bank	380	
	1,980	
Current liabilities		
Creditors (W5)	280	
Dividend to minority interest: 80 × 25%	20	
Proposed dividend	280	
Corporation tax	280	
	860	
Net current assets		1,120
		2,818
Capital and reserves		
Share capital: £1 ordinary shares		1,800
Profit and loss account (W7)		838
		2,638
Minority interest (W6)		180
		2,818

Workings

1   *Group structure*

Lawton

$\downarrow \dfrac{300}{400} = 75\%$

Doig

2 *Turnover and cost of sales*

	Turnover		Cost of sales	
	£'000	£'000	£'000	£'000
Lawton per question	3,400			2,300
Less intercompany				
(300 × 120/100)	360			
		3,040		2,300
Doig per question		1,200	820	
Less intercompany			(360)	
				460
		4,240		2,760

3 *Investment income*

	£'000
Lawton per question	64
Less dividend from Doig: 75% × 80	60
	4

4 *Unamortised goodwill*

	£'000
Goodwill per question	95
Less 3 years' amortisation: 95 × 3/5	57
Unamortised goodwill	38

5 *Debtors and creditors*

	Debtors	Creditors
	£'000	£'000
Lawton	540	180
Doig	280	140
Less intercompany sale	(40)	(40)
Intercompany dividends (W3)	(60)	–
	720	280

6 *Minority interest*

Doig: net assets at balance sheet date

	£'000
Share capital	400
Profit and loss account	320
	720

∴ Minority interest: £720,000 × 25% = £180,000

7   *Profit and loss account*

	Lawton £'000	Doig £'000
Per question	760	320
Pre-acquisition		140
		180
Share of Doig: 75% × 180	135	
Goodwill amortised (W4)	(57)	
	838	

Part B

TASK 1.2

KENTISH LIMITED
PROFIT AND LOSS ACCOUNT FOR THE YEAR ENDED 31 DECEMBER 20X3

	£'000	£'000
Turnover		
Continuing operations	63,972	
		63,972
Cost of sales (W1)		28,149
Gross profit		35,823
Distribution costs		10,245
Administrative expenses		7,821
Operating profit		
Continuing operations	17,757	
Profit on ordinary activities before interest		17,757
Interest payable (W2)		1,080
Profit on ordinary activities before taxation		16,677
Tax on profit on ordinary activities		4,701
Profit on ordinary activities after taxation		11,976
Dividends (W3)		2,025
Retained profit for the financial year		9,951

Workings

1   *Cost of sales*

	£'000
Opening stock	9,381
Purchases	34,743
Carriage inwards	249
	44,373
Less closing stock	16,224
	28,149

2   *Interest payable*

	£'000
Per trial balance	540
Plus accrual 12,000 × 9% × 6/12	540
	1,080

3   *Dividends*

	£'000
Interim	900
Final: 7,500 × 15p	1,125
	2,025

TASK 1.3

KENTISH LIMITED
NOTE OF HISTORICAL COST PROFITS AND LOSSES
FOR THE YEAR ENDED 31 DECEMBER 20X3

	£'000
Reported profit on ordinary activities before taxation	16,677
Difference between historical cost depreciation and the actual depreciation charge of the year calculated on the revalued amount (216 – 186)	30
Historical cost profit on ordinary activities before taxation	16,707
Historical cost retained profit (9,951 + 30)	9,981

TASK 1.4

ABC Accountants
1 Any Road
Anytown
AN1 7UN

The Directors
Kentish Ltd
Anytown
AN1 7UX

Dear Sirs (Directors)

(a) **Ordinary share capital**

This is the most common type of share capital. Ordinary shareholders are in effect the **owners** of a company. They own the equity and the reserves.

Ordinary shares carry **no right to a fixed dividend** but are entitled to all profits left after payment of any preference dividend.

Should the company be wound up, any surplus not distributed is shared between the ordinary shareholders. Ordinary shares **normally carry voting rights**.

(b) **Preference share capital**

Preference shares are shares which confer certain preferential rights on their holder. They carry the **right to a fixed dividend** which is expressed as a percentage of their nominal value. Preference dividends have priority over ordinary dividends; in other words if the directors of a company wish to pay a dividend they must pay any preference dividend first.

The rights attaching to preference shares vary according to the company's constitution. Generally preference shares **do not carry a right to vote**. They may give a priority right to a **return of capital** if the company goes into liquidation.

Yours sincerely

A Technician

Part C

TASK 1.5

(a)   EVANS LIMITED
CASH FLOW STATEMENT FOR THE YEAR ENDED 31 OCTOBER 20X1

Reconciliation of operating profit to net cash inflow from operating activities

	£'000	£'000
Operating profit (418 + 35 – 12)		441
Depreciation		
Vehicles (W)	120	
Furniture (270 – 200)	70	
		190
Gain on disposal		(10)
Decrease in stock (505 – 486)		19
Increase in debtors (790 – 577)		(213)
Increase in creditors (560 – 46)		14
Net cash inflow from operating activities		441

Cash flow statement

	£'000	£'000
Net cash inflow from operating activities		441
Returns on investments and servicing of finance		
Dividend received	12	
Interest paid	(35)	
		(23)
Taxation		
Corporation tax paid		(106)
Capital expenditure		
Payments to acquire fixed assets (W)	(425)	
Payments to acquire investments (155 – 80)	(75)	
Proceeds from sale of fixed assets	75	
		(425)
		(113)
Equity dividends paid		(40)
		(153)
Financing		
Issue of share capital (1,200 – 1,000)	200	
Share premium (315 – 270)	45	
Repayment of debentures (150 – 50)	(100)	
		145
Decrease in cash		(8)

Notes to the cash flow statement

1   *Reconciliation of net cash flow to movement in net debt*

	£'000
Net cash outflow for the period	(8)
Decrease in long-term loan	100
Change in net debt	92
Net debt at 1 November 20X0	(140)
Net debt at 31 October 20X1	(48)

2   *Analysis of changes in net debt*

	At 1 November 20X0 £'000	Cash flows £'000	At 31 October 20X1 £'000
Cash at bank	10	(8)	2
Debt due after one year	(150)	100	(50)
	(140)	92	(48)

Working: fixed assets and depreciation

VEHICLES: COST

	£'000		£'000
Balance b/f	820	Disposals	155
Additions (bal fig)	225	Balance c/f	890
	1,045		1,045

VEHICLES: ACCUMULATED DEPRECIATION

	£'000		£'000
Disposals (155 – 65)	90	Balance b/f	310
Balance c/f	340	P&L charge (bal fig)	120
	430		430

VEHICLES: DISPOSALS

	£'000		£'000
Fixed assets	155	Accumulated depn	90
Gain on disposal	10	Sale proceeds (bal fig)	75
	165		165

Additions to fixed assets:

	£'000
Vehicles	225
Furniture (900 – 700)	200
	425

(b)   While the profit and loss account and balance sheet provide useful information to outside users, it could be argued that the profit figure in the accounts does not always give a meaningful picture of the company's operations. A company's performance and prospects depend not so much on the 'profits' earned in the period, but, more realistically on **liquidity** or cash flows.

Cash flow statements have the **following advantages**.

(i) They are **easier to understand** than profit statements.

(ii) They draw attention to **cash flow** which is **crucial to a business's survival**.

(iii) **Creditors** are more interested in a company's **ability to pay** the debt than in profitability.

(iv) **Profit** depends on **accounting conventions** and concepts and is thus easy to manipulate.

(v) **Management decision making** is based on future cash flows.

(vi) Cash flow is easier to audit than profit.

Section 2

Part A

TASK 2.1

REPORT

To: Michael Beacham
From: Accounting Technician
Date: 23 June 20X2

Subject: Analysis of performance of Goodall Ltd

Introduction

The aim of this report is to help you decide whether or not to lend money to Goodall Ltd. The report explains the meaning of the ratios calculated for you by your financial adviser. In addition, it analyses the financial position and performance of the company over the years 20X1 and 20X2 and compares the results with the industry average.

Explanation and discussion of ratios

Gearing ratio

This ratio measures the percentage of debt capital to total capital employed. The ratio is **higher** in 20X2 than in 20X1 and is also considerably higher than the industry average (more than half as much again).

As we are considering lending money to Goodall Ltd, we should be very wary of any factors which suggest that it may not be able to continue in business. High gearing is one such factor. Large debts carry a **risk of insolvency** and the company may have **difficulty meeting interest payments**.

Interest cover

This is the ratio of operating profit to interest. It shows whether a company is earning enough profits before interest and tax to pay its interest costs comfortably, or whether its interest costs are high in relation to the size of its profits. **Low levels of cover make it difficult for a company to borrow more funds, and make the company riskier to lend to.**

The interest cover of Goodall Ltd has more or less halved between 20X1 and 20X2, and it is only around a quarter of the industry average. This should give rise to concern.

Quick ratio/acid test

This ratio shows how many assets, excluding stock, are available to meet current liabilities. Stock is excluded because it is not always readily convertible into cash. The quick ratio or acid test is therefore a better indicator of a company's true liquidity than the current ratio which does not exclude stock.

Goodall Ltd's ratio has declined from a low base in 20X1, and is considerably lower than the industry average. We do not have a breakdown between cash and debtors, but this ratio suggests **liquidity problems**.

Return on equity

The return on equity measures the percentage of profit available for equity shareholders that is generated by the use of equity finance. The ratio has **declined** this year compared to 20X1, and is less than half the industry average. This makes it a less attractive investment prospect than other companies in the sector. This impacts on the decision to lend money, since the company is less likely to find sources of funding elsewhere to help solve its liquidity problems.

Conclusion

Goodall Ltd is a **high risk investment**. It is highly geared, and the gearing ratio is rising. It has liquidity problems in the short term, as shown by the quick ratio, and is storing up problems in the long term as regards payment of interest. Furthermore, the company does not appear to be giving a good return to equity investors, which would lessen the risk for loan creditors.

We do not have any figures for turnover and profits, which would tell us whether some of the problems were due to rapid growth. Nevertheless, it is safe to say that this company would be **too risky** to lend money too at the moment.

Part B

TASK 2.2

(a) The *Statement of Principles* objective has been met in that Michael and his advisers are **users** of financial statements. Specifically they are potential lenders, one of the groups identified by the *Statement*. Lenders need to know the financial position of a business in order to judge security and the ability of the business to repay the interest or capital. Decisions are also needed regarding the ability of a business to handle an increase level of borrowings.

From another standpoint, the information helped Michael **make an economic decision** about whether to lend the money.

(b) The elements 'assets', 'liabilities' and 'ownership interest' are shown in the **balance sheet.** They are related in the balance sheet by the **accounting equation** as follows.

Assets less liabilities = ownership interest.

(c) The *Statement of Principles* defines **gains** as:

'increases in ownership interest not resulting from contributions from owners'.

The *Statement* defines **losses** as:

'decreases in ownership interest not resulting from distributions to owners'.

Both gains and losses are shown either in the **profit and loss account**, or the **statement of total recognised gains and losses.**

DECEMBER 2002 EXAM PAPER

ANSWERS

DO NOT TURN THIS PAGE UNTIL YOU HAVE COMPLETED THE EXAM

Section 1

Part A

TASK 1.1

SUGAR PLC
CONSOLIDATED PROFIT AND LOSS ACCOUNT
FOR THE YEAR ENDED 31 OCTOBER 20X2

	£'000
Turnover (W3)	3,635
Cost of sales (bal fig)	2,067
Gross profit (W4)	1,568
Distribution costs	690
Administrative expenses	420
Amortisation of goodwill (W1)	80
Profit on ordinary activities before taxation	378
Tax on profit on ordinary activities	210
Profit on ordinary activities after taxation	168
Minority interests ($105 \times 20\%$)	(21)
Group profit for the year	147
Proposed dividends	(100)
Retained profit for the year	47
Retained profits brought forward (W2)	215
Retained profits carried forward	262

Workings

1 *Goodwill*

	£'000	£'000
Cost of investment		2,100
Share of net assets acquired		
Share capital	2,000	
Profit and loss account	125	
	2,125	
Group share: 80%		1,700
Goodwill		400

Annual charge to profit and loss account $\dfrac{£400,000}{5} = £80,000$

PROFESSIONAL EDUCATION

2   *Retained profits brought forward*

	Sugar £'000	Spice £'000
Per question	275	150
Pre acquisition		125
		25
Share of Spice: 25 × 80%	20	
Goodwill amortised at 31 October 20X1		
(1 year − see (W1)	(80)	
	215	

3   *Turnover*

	£'000
Sugar	2,800
Spice	1,000
	3,800
Less intercompany	165
	3,635

4   *Gross profit*

	£'000
Sugar	1,150
Spice	450
Less provision for unrealised profit: (165,000 − 85,000) × 40%	(32)
	1,568

Note. Because the intercompany sale was made by the parent company, the whole of the unrealised profit must be eliminated.

Part B

TASK 1.2

QUINE LIMITED
BALANCE SHEET AS AT 30 SEPTEMBER 20X2

	£'000	£'000
Fixed assets		
Intangible asset: development expenditure		840
Tangible assets (W1)		5,300
		6,140
Current assets		
Stocks	2,382	
Debtors (W2)	1,814	
Bank	103	
	4,299	
Creditors: amounts falling due within one year (W3)	2,262	
		2,037
		8,177
Creditors: amounts falling due after one year		
Long-term loan		2,500
		5,677
Capital and reserves		
Called up share capital (£1 shares)		3,000
Share premium		500
Revaluation reserve (W4)		400
Profit and loss account (W5)		1,777
		5,677

Workings

1   *Fixed assets*

	Cost/val'n	Accum dep'n	NBV
	£'000	£'000	£'000
Land	3,200		3,200
Buildings	1,480	702	778
Fixtures and fittings	645	317	328
Motor vehicles	1,632	903	729
Office equipment	447	182	265
	7,404	2,104	5,300

2   *Debtors*

	£'000
Trade debtors per trial balance	1,802
Less provision for doubtful debts	(72)
	1,730
Prepayments	84
	1,814

3 *Creditors: amounts falling due within one year*

	£'000
Trade creditors	1,309
Accruals	105
Corporation tax payable	548
Dividends payable (3,000 × 10p)	300
	2,262

4 *Revaluation reserve*

	£'000
Fair value of land	3,200
Cost	2,800
Revaluation reserve	400

5 *Profit and loss account*

	£'000
Per trial balance	2,625
Less proposed dividend (W3)	(300)
Less corporation tax	(548)
	1,777

TASK 1.3

NOTES FOR MEETING WITH THE CHIEF ACCOUNTANT

(a) Following FRS 18 *Accounting policies,* Quine Ltd should have regard to the following in selecting accounting policies.

    (i) The requirements of **accounting standards** (financial reporting standards issued by the Accounting Standards Board and statements of standard accounting practice issued by the old Accounting Standards Committee)

    (ii) Abstracts issued by the **Urgent Issues Task Force**

    (iii) **Companies legislation**

There is an **overriding requirement** for financial statements to give a **true and fair view.** Where compliance with accounting standards or UITF abstracts is inconsistent with this requirement, they should be departed from to the extent necessary to give a true and fair view.

(b) The **four objectives** set out in FRS 18 are:

    (i) Relevance
    (ii) Reliability
    (iii) Comparability
    (iv) Understandability

(c) The two '**bedrock**' **concepts** in FRS 18 are:

- Going concern
- Accruals

Prudence is a less important concept than it was under the old SSAP 2, which FRS 18 replaced.

Part C

TASK 1.4

NEWTON LIMITED
CASH FLOW STATEMENT
FOR THE YEAR ENDED 31 DECEMBER 20X9

Reconciliation of operating profit to net cash flows from operating activities

	£'000
Profit before interest and tax (2,440 + 235)	2,675
Depreciation (W)	2,640
Loss on disposal	250
Increase in stock (4,217 – 2,695)	(1,522)
Increase in debtors (2,500 – 1,740)	(760)
Increase in creditors (3,290 – 2,065)	1,225
Net cash inflow from operating activities	4,508

Cash flow statement

	£'000	£'000
Net cash inflow from operating activities		4,508
Returns on investments and servicing of finance		
Interest paid		(235)
Taxation		
Corporation tax paid		(400)
Capital expenditure		
Payments to acquire fixed assets (W)	(5,518)	
Proceeds from sale of fixed assets	500	
		(5,018)
		(1,145)
Equity dividends paid		(30)
Financing		
Issue of share capital (1,235 – 795)	440	
Share premium (650 – 495)	155	
Long term loans (1,145 – 875)	270	
		865
Decrease in cash		(310)

Notes to the cash flow statement

1   *Reconciliation of net cash flow to movement in net debt*

	£'000
Net cash outflow for the period	(310)
Increase in long term loans	(270)
Change in net debt	(580)
Net debt at 1 January 20X9	(985)
Net debt at 31 December 20X9	(1,565)

2   *Analysis of changes in net debt*

	At 1 Jan 20X9 £'000	Cash flows £'000	At 31 Dec 20X9 £'000
Bank overdraft	(110)	(310)	(420)
Debt due after 1 year	(875)	(270)	(1,145)
	(985)	(580)	(1,565)

Working: fixed assets and depreciation

FIXED ASSETS: COST

	£'000		£'000
Balance b/f	6,545	Disposals	2,500
Additions	5,518	Balance c/f	9,563
	12,063		12,063

FIXED ASSETS: ACCUMULATED DEPRECIATION

	£'000		£'000
Disposals	1,750	Balance b/f	5,120
Balance c/f	6,010	P & L a/c (bal. fig.)	2,640
	7,760		7,760

FIXED ASSETS: DISPOSALS

	£'000		£'000
Disposals	2,500	Accumulated depn. (2,500 – 750)	1,750
		Sale proceeds	500
		Loss on disposal (balance figure)	250
	2,500		2,500

Section 2

TASK 2.1

Accounting Technician
2 Any Street
Anytown
NE1 2RY

Karel Popper
Zipps Ltd
6 Garment Street
Anytown
NE4 6JZ
20 December 20X2

Dear Mr Popper

Liquidity and Financial Position of Zipps Ltd

I am writing in response to your request for an analysis of the financial statements of Zipps Ltd. The emphasis of my analysis will be the issue of whether the bank is likely to lend money to the company. My analysis is based solely on the financial statements of the business for the two years 20X1 and 20X2, and on the ratios calculated from those financial statements. The calculation of the ratios is shown in the Appendix to this letter.

Current ratio

This is a liquidity ratio, showing the extent to which a company's current liabilities are covered by current assets. Generally speaking, a current ratio of less than one gives cause for concern – if a company cannot pay its creditors, it may go out of business.

The company's current ratio is **healthy** at 2.2:1, and has shown an increase on the previous year (2.1:1). However, the cash balance has gone down, so the liquidity is not as good as it might be. A better test of liquidity is the acid test ratio.

Quick ratio/acid test

The quick ratio shows how many assets, excluding stock, are available to meet the current liabilities. Stock is excluded because it is not always readily convertible into cash. The quick ratio or acid test is therefore a better indicator of a company's true liquidity than the current ratio which does not exclude stock.

Zipps' ratio has **declined**, albeit by a very small amount (from 1.1:1 to 0.9:1). In 20X1 the company had more than enough assets to cover its liabilities, whereas in 20X2 there is a shortfall. The increase in the current ratio is due to an increase in stock, the least liquid of the current assets.

Gearing ratio

As the bank will be considering whether to lend money to Zipps Ltd, it will be very wary of any factors which suggest that the company may not be able to continue in business. High gearing is one such factor. Large debts carry **risk of insolvency** and the company may have difficulty meeting interest payments.

The gearing ratio can be calculated in two ways: debt/equity and debt/capital employed. Gint's ratio, whichever way it is calculated, has **risen** compared with 20X1. Calculated as debt to equity, there is an increase of 86%, which is considerable. Calculated as debt to shareholders' funds the increase is smaller, though still material (50% to 65%). It is likely that the bank will consider the company **high risk**.

BPP
PROFESSIONAL EDUCATION

Interest cover

The interest cover ratio shows whether a company is earning enough profits before interest and tax to pay its interest costs comfortably, or whether its interest costs are high in relation to the size of its profits. Low levels of cover may make it difficult for a company to borrow more funds. Ordinary shareholders are unlikely to invest further in a company whose profits are reduced by interest costs leaving no return for them.

The company's interest cover has decreased significantly from 3.5 times to −0.4 times. There are **no profits available to cover interest payments.**

Further information

In addition to the ratios calculated, it is worth noting that **turnover and profits are both down,** and that the company has gone from an operating profit of £270,000 to an operating loss of £46,000. It looks as if costs are not being controlled, since both cost of sales and expenses have risen. It might be worth looking into why: has the company spent money on advertising for, example? Fixed assets have gone up: is the company trying to expand?

Conclusion

The bank is likely to focus on the interest cover and the gearing ratio. If interest payments are unlikely to be met, it will not lend money to the company unless there are credible indications that profits are very likely to rise in the future. Analysis of the ratios would not persuade the bank to lend money.

The company is highly geared, so a loan to the company would be risky, especially as liquidity is poor. In conclusion, it is **unlikely that the bank would lend money** to the company at the present time.

Yours sincerely

A Technician

APPENDIX: CALCULATION OF RATIOS

Ratios	*20X2*	*20X1*
Current ratio = $\dfrac{\text{Current assets}}{\text{Current liabilities}}$	$\dfrac{1{,}430}{650} = 2.2:1$	$\dfrac{1{,}302}{620} = 2.1:1$
Quick ratio (acid test) = $\dfrac{\text{Current assets less stocks}}{\text{Current liabilities}}$	$\dfrac{585}{650} = 0.9:1$	$\dfrac{682}{620} = 1.1:1$
Gearing ratio = $\dfrac{\text{Long-term debts}}{\text{Long term debt} + \text{Ordinary shareholders' funds}}$	$\dfrac{1{,}300}{2{,}000} = 65\%$	$\dfrac{900}{1{,}800} = 50\%$
[alternative ratio]		
Debt/equity ratio = $\dfrac{\text{Long-term debt}}{\text{Ordinary shareholders' funds}}$	$\dfrac{1{,}300}{700} = 186\%$	$\dfrac{900}{900} = 100\%$
Interest cover = $\dfrac{\text{Profit/(loss) before interest and tax}}{\text{Interest charges}}$	$\dfrac{(46)}{104} = -0.4$ times	$\dfrac{270}{77} = 3.5$ times

TASK 2.2

(a) According to the *Statement of Principles,* management, in its **stewardship** role, is accountable for the safekeeping of a company's resources and for their efficient and profitable use. Potential investors are interested in information that enables them to assess how effectively management has fulfilled this role. They are also interested in information that is useful in taking decisions about their potential investment in the company.

As a result, potential investors will want to know how **profitable** the company is, as determined by the **performance statements** (profit and loss account and statement of total recognised gains and losses). They will also be interested in the company's ability to **generate cash flows**, and such information can be gleaned from the **cash flow statement**. The **financial structure** of the company, for example, its **gearing**, will tell the potential investor how **risky** the company is.

(b) The *Statement of Principles* defines **asset**s as 'rights or access to **future economic benefits** controlled by an entity as a result of **past transactions** or events'. Considering each aspect in turn:

(i) Stock gives rights to **future economic benefits** controlled by the entity because it will be **sold for cash** at some time in the future.

(ii) The **past transaction** giving rise to the asset was the **purchase of stock** by the company.

Answers to AAT
Specimen Exam

AAT SPECIMEN EXAM PAPER

ANSWERS

DO NOT TURN THIS PAGE UNTIL YOU HAVE COMPLETED THE EXAM

Section 1

Part A

TASK 1.1

JAKE LIMITED
CONSOLIDATED BALANCE SHEET AS AT 30 SEPTEMBER 20X1

	£'000	£'000
Fixed assets		
Intangible: goodwill (W2)		477
Tangible (18,104 + 6,802 + 600) (W2)		25,506
		25,983
Current assets (4,852 + 2,395)	7,247	
Current liabilities (2,376 + 547)	2,923	
Net current assets		4,324
Total assets less current liabilities		30,307
Long-term loan (4,500 + 1,000)		5,500
		24,807
Capital and reserves		
Share capital		5,000
Share premium		3,000
Profit and loss account (W4)		13,507
		21,507
Minority interests (W3)		3,300
		24,807

Workings

1   *Group structure*

Jake

$$\frac{600,000}{1,000,000} = 60\%$$

Dinos

∴ Minority interest = 40%

2   *Goodwill*

	£'000	£'000
Cost of investment		5,000
Share of net assets acquired		
Share capital	1,000	
Share premium	400	
Profit and loss account	5,450	
Revaluation reserve (3,652 – 3,052)	600	
	7,450	
Group share: 60%		4,470
Goodwill		530
Less one year's amortisation (530/10)		53
		477

3   *Minority interest*

	£'000
Net assets of Dinos Ltd	
Per question	7,650
Revaluation	600
	8,250

∴ Minority interests = £8,250,000 × 40% = £3,300,000

4   *Profit and loss account*

	Jake	Dinos
	£'000	£'000
Per question	13,080	6,250
Pre-acquisition		(5,450)
Share of Dinos		800
800 × 60%	480	
Less goodwill amortised (W3)	(53)	
	13,507	

TASK 1.2

(a)   The treatment of goodwill arising on consolidation is governed by FRS 10 *Goodwill and intangible assets*. The FRS states that if goodwill is regarded as having an indefinite useful economic life, it should **not be amortised**.

(b)   If goodwill is not amortised then it should be shown **at cost** in the balance sheet. An **impairment review** should be carried out each year in accordance with FRS 11 *Impairment of fixed assets and goodwill*. If any impairment has occurred, the goodwill should be written down to the recoverable amount, where this is below the carrying amount.

Part B

TASK 1.3

		£'000	£'000
DEBIT	Dividends (P&L) (4,000 × 15p)	600	
CREDIT	Dividends proposed		600
DEBIT	Stock (balance sheet)	7,878	
CREDIT	Stock (profit and loss account)		7,878
DEBIT	Tax charge	1,920	
CREDIT	Tax payable		1,920
DEBIT	Sales	204	
CREDIT	Debtors		204
DEBIT	Interest (profit and loss account) (W)	240	
CREDIT	Interest payable		240

Working: interest

Interest for year @ 8%   = 8% × £6,000,000
                          = £480,000

∴ Six months' interest accrued   = £480,000 × 6/12
                                   = £240,000

TASK 1.4

HIGHTINK LIMITED
PROFIT AND LOSS ACCOUNT
FOR THE YEAR ENDED 30 SEPTEMBER 20X2

	£'000	£'000
Turnover		
Continuing operations	31,506	
		31,506
Cost of sales (W2)		14,178
Gross profit		17,328
Distribution costs	6,852	
Administration expenses	3,378	
Operating profit		
Continuing operations	7,098	
Profit on ordinary activities before interest		7,098
Interest payable and similar charges (Task 1.3)		(480)
Profit on ordinary activities before taxation		6,618
Tax on profit on ordinary activities		(1,920)
Profit on ordinary activities after taxation		4,698
Dividends (W3)		(1,000)
Retained profit for the financial year		3,698

Workings

		£'000
1	*Turnover*	
	Per trial balance	31,710
	Less credit sales wrongly included	204
		31,506

		£'000
2	*Cost of sales*	
	Opening stock	6,531
	Purchases	15,525
		22,056
	Less closing stock	(7,878)
		14,178

		£'000
3	*Dividends*	
	Interim dividend 4,000 × 10p	400
	Final dividend 4,000 × 15p	600
		1,000

TASK 1.5

MEMO

To: The Directors, Hightink Ltd
Date: 1 November 20X2

Subject: Post balance sheet events

(a) Events after the balance sheet date may affect the position at the balance sheet date. Post balance sheet events are defined in SSAP 17 *Accounting for post balance sheet events*. They are:

> 'events, both favourable and unfavourable, which **occur between the balance sheet date and the date on which the financial statements are approved by the directors**'.

(b) SSAP 17 makes a distinction between **adjusting events** and **non-adjusting events.**

   (i) **Adjusting events** are post balance sheet events which provide additional evidence of conditions existing at the balance sheet date. They include events which, because of statutory or conventional requirements, are reflected in the financial statements.

   (ii) **Non-adjusting events** are events which arise after the balance sheet date and concern conditions which did not exist at that time. They do not result in changes in amounts in financial statements, but must be disclosed if material.

(c) The loss resulting from the fire at the company's premises on 21 October 20X2 is a **non-adjusting event.** It is one of the examples of non-adjusting events given in SSAP 17. The condition **did not exist at the balance sheet date** and so does **not result in changes** to the financial statements. However, the event is clearly highly **material**, and so must be **disclosed by way of a note** in order to ensure that financial statements are not misleading.

Part C

TASK 1.6

STRINGBERG LIMITED
RECONCILIATION OF OPERATING PROFIT
TO NET CASH INFLOW FROM OPERATING ACTIVITIES
FOR THE YEAR ENDED 31 MARCH 20X1

	£'000
Operating activities	2,466
Add back depreciation	505
Deduct profit on sale of tangible fixed assets	(93)
Increase in stocks (3,016 – 2,284)	(732)
Increase in debtors (1,508 – 1,394))	(114)
Increase in creditors (1,372 – 930)	442
Net cash inflow from operating activities	2,474

TASK 1.7

STRINGBERG LIMITED
CASH FLOW STATEMENT FOR THE YEAR ENDED 31 MARCH 20X1

	£'000	£'000
Net cash inflow from operating activities		2,474
Returns on investments and servicing of finance		
Interest paid		(243)
Taxation		(492)
Capital expenditure		
Payments to acquire tangible fixed assets (W1)	(1,986)	
Proceeds from sale of fixed asset (W1)	283	
		(1,703)
		36
Equity dividends paid		(590)
		(554)
Financing		
Loan (3,324 – 3,038)	(286)	
Issue of share capital (2,500 – 1,900)	600	
Share premium	400	
		714
Increase in cash		160

Workings

1   *Fixed assets*

FIXED ASSETS

	£'000		£'000
Balance b/fwd (NBV)	4,075	Depreciation	505
Additions (bal fig)	1,986	Disposal (363 – 173)	190
		Balance c/fwd (NBV)	5,366
	6,061		6,061

Disposal proceeds:

	£'000
NBV of asset sold	190
Profit on sale	93
∴ Proceeds	283

2   *Dividends*

DIVIDENDS

	£'000		£'000
Cash paid (bal. fig.)	590	Balance b/f	380
Balance c/f	420	Profit and loss	630
	1,010		1,010

Section 2

TASK 2.1

REPORT

To: Jack Matease
From: A Technician
Date: December 20X1

Subject: Financial Statements of Fauve Ltd

The purpose of this report is to assist you in interpreting the financial statements of Fauve Ltd and to help you decide whether to invest in the company. The report is in three parts:

(a)   Calculation of key ratios
(b)   Explanation of the meaning of each ratio and application to Fauve Ltd
(c)   A conclusion regarding overall performance of the company

(a)   **Calculation of ratios**

	20X1	20X0
Return on capital employed	$\frac{1,251}{8,430} = 14.8\%$	$\frac{624}{5,405} = 11.5\%$
Net profit percentage	$\frac{1,251}{4,315} = 29\%$	$\frac{624}{2,973} = 21\%$
Expenses to sales*	$\frac{1,554}{4,315} = 36\%$	$\frac{1,160}{2,973} = 39\%$
Gross profit percentage	$\frac{2,805}{4,315} = 65\%$	$\frac{1,784}{2,973} = 60\%$
Asset turnover	$\frac{4,315}{8,430} = 0.51$	$\frac{2,973}{5,405} = 0.55$

* *Note.* You were not asked specifically for this, but it will be useful for your explanation.

(b)   **Explanations and comment**

Return on capital employed

This ratio states the profit as a percentage of the amount of capital employed. It is calculated as:

$$\frac{\text{Profit before interest and taxation}}{\text{Capital employed}}$$

Capital employed is calculated here as shareholders' funds plus long-term loan.

The calculation shows that the ratio has **increased** in 20X1, as compared with 20X0. This is a good sign, particularly as profit has more than doubled in absolute terms, showing that the margin has been maintained even though the company is expanding.

Net profit percentage

This ratio states the net profit as a percentage of sales. It is calculated as:

$$\frac{\text{Net profit}}{\text{Sales}}$$

This ratio shows an **increase** in 20X1 over 20X0. This could be because the gross profit margin has increased, or because expenses have decreased relative to sales, or both. Interestingly, the ratio of expenses to sales has also gone down from 39% in 20X0 to 36% in 20X1.

Gross profit percentage

Calculated as gross profit/sales, this ratio shows the gross profit margin on sales. There has been an increase from 60% in 20X0 to 65% in 20X1. It is a good sign, that although the company is expanding both sales and profits, this is not at the expense of a favourable profit margin.

The margin has **increased** because cost of sales has not increased in proportion to sales. Perhaps the company is benefiting from economies of scale.

Asset turnover

This a measure of how efficient the company is. It shows how effectively it generates sales from the capital employed or net assets.

There has been a **slight deterioration** in asset turnover in 20X1 as opposed to 20X0. However, this is not necessarily a cause for concern. If you compare the fixed assets and current assets figures in the balance sheets you will see that the company has invested heavily in fixed assets in order to expand. It is possible that these fixed assets will produce higher revenues and profits in the future.

(c) Conclusion on overall performance

The financial statements and ratios indicate that this company is a good one to invest in. **Turnover** and **profits are expanding rapidly, but not at the expense of profit margin** and expenses are being kept firmly under control. There is a slight deterioration in efficiency as measured by asset turnover, which should correct itself as the company continues to expand and as the investment in fixed and current assets pays off.

I hope you find this analysis useful

A Technician

TASK 2.2

Notes for Meeting with Jack Matease

(a) **Assets** are defined in the ASB's *Statement of Principles* as 'rights or other access to future economic benefits controlled by an entity as a result of past transactions or events'. Each part of this definition can be applied to the plant and machinery as follows.

(i) The company has rights and access to any **future economic benefits** generated by the products manufactured by the plant and machinery.

(ii) The company **controls** the plant and machinery and has right to use it.

(iii) There has been a **past transaction,** namely the purchase of the plant and machinery.

(b) **Liabilities** are also defined by the *Statement of Principles*. The definition is, 'obligations of an entity to **transfer economic benefits** as a result of past transaction or events'. This definition can be applied to the bank loan as follows.

    (i) The entity has an **obligation to transfer economic benefits** in the future in that the loan must be repaid and interest must be paid on the loan.

    (ii) The obligation arose as a result of a **past transaction**, namely the receipt of money from the bank.

(c) (i) The figure of 'retained profit for the year' relates only to the current year. The **retained profit figure in the balance sheet represents the accumulated profits from previous years** insofar as they have not been distributed as dividends.

    (ii) The two are **connected.** The profit for the year in the profit and loss account is added to the profits brought forward from previous years. The total is the retained profits carried forward which is shown in the balance sheet.

Lecturers' Resource Pack Activities

Note to Students

The answers to these activities and assessments are provided to your lecturers, who will distribute them in class.

If you are not on a classroom based course, a copy of the answers can be obtained from Customer Services on 020 8740 2211 or e-mail publishing @bpp.com.

Note to Lecturers

The answers to these activities and assessments are included in the Lecturers' Resource Pack, provided free to colleges.

If your college has not received the Lecturers' Resource Pack, please contact Customer Services on 020 8740 2211 or e-mail publishing @bpp.com.

Lecturers' Practice Activities

Chapters 1 and 2 Introduction; Accounting conventions

1 Assets

(a) Explain the following terms:

Fixed asset
Current asset
Current liability

(b) Under what circumstances should a fixed asset be recognised in the financial statements of an entity?

(c) Explain how items which have been hired by a business should be recognised in the financial statements.

(25 mins)

2 Primary financial statements

(a) Identify the primary financial statements which a business produces.

(b) Explain the links between the primary financial statements.

(c) Discuss the relevance of the primary financial statements to a large charitable organisation (constituted as a limited company).

(d) Discuss the extent to which the primary financial statements produced by a business will satisfy the information needs of a member of the public.

(25 mins)

Chapters 3 to 9 Limited companies

3 Woodpecker

You are working in the business services department of a firm of accountants. A client of the firm, Woodpecker Ltd, a wholesale builders' merchant, has recently lost its financial accountant and has asked the firm to provide assistance in drafting the financial statements of the company for the year ended 31 March 20X4. The accountant who left the company has produced an extended trial balance, which includes some of the normal year end adjustments, and gathered some further information which may be relevant to the year end accounts. You have been asked by one of the partners of the firm to take on the task.

The extended trial balance of Woodpecker Ltd is set out on page 196. The following further information is provided.

(a)   The authorised share capital of the company is as follows.

   4,000,000 ordinary shares of 25p each
   500,000 10% preference shares of £1.00 each

   At the beginning of the year 1,600,000 shares were in issue (all were fully paid). A further 800,000 shares were issued during the year at a price of 75p per share. The whole of the proceeds of the issue, which were received in full, was credited to the ordinary share capital account.

(b)   The directors decided that instead of paying a dividend to ordinary shareholders they would make a bonus issue of shares at the year end. Ordinary shareholders received one ordinary share of 25p for every six ordinary shares held by them at the year end. No entries have been made in the extended trial balance to reflect this issue.

(c)   The interim dividend in the trial balance represents a dividend paid to preference shareholders. It has been decided to provide for the full preference dividend in the year end accounts but no entry has yet been made to reflect this decision.

(d)   No interest on the debentures has been paid during the year or provided for in the extended trial balance.

(e)   The investment property shown in the extended trial balance at a value of £800,000 represents an office building purchased by the company as an investment. It has been revalued by J Wheeler and Co, a firm of chartered surveyors, at £600,000 based on its value given its current use. The valuation has not been reflected in the extended trial balance.

(f)   Audit fees of £25,000 have not been paid or provided for in the extended trial balance.

(g)   The corporation tax charge for the year has been calculated as £275,000.

(h)   The balance on the goodwill account arose out of the purchase of an unincorporated business some years ago. The goodwill was purchased at a cost of £50,000 and is being amortised over ten years. No entry has been made for the amortisation of goodwill for the year ended 31 March 20X4.

(i)   The remuneration of the directors for the year was as follows.

	£
Chairman	31,000
Sales director	42,000
Executive director	56,000

The remuneration of the directors is included in the salaries and wages figure in the extended trial balance. The directors' fees and pension contributions made on behalf of the directors are made up as follows.

	Fees	Pension contributions
	£	£
Chairman	2,000	4,000
Sales director	2,000	5,000
Executive director	3,000	6,000
	7,000	15,000

The two directors other than the sales director work on general administration.

(j) For the purposes of the published financial statements the following allocation of expenses is to be made.

	Distribution costs	Administrative expenses
	£'000	£'000
Motor expenses	47	31
Light and heat	20	6
Insurance	29	9
General expenses	186	48
Depreciation of motor vehicles	151	38
Depreciation of office equipment	22	15
Depreciation of buildings	16	5
Depreciation of fixtures and fittings	65	-

Salaries and wages, excluding directors' remuneration, are to be allocated on the basis of 75% to the distribution department and 25% to the administration department.

(k) All the operations of the company are continuing operations.

Tasks

(a) Make any adjustments you feel to be necessary to the balances in the extended trial balance as a result of the matters set out in the further information above. Set out your adjustments in the form of journal entries. (Ignore any effect of these adjustments on the tax charge for the year as given above.)   (16 mins)
No narratives are required for the journal entries.

(b) (i) Draft a profit and loss account for the year ended 31 March 20X4 and a balance sheet as at that date in a form suitable for publication using Format 1 in accordance with the Companies Act 1985 as supplemented by FRS 3 Reporting financial performance. (You are not required to prepare a statement of total recognised gains and losses or the reconciliation of movements in shareholders' funds required under FRS 3.)

   (ii) Provide suitable notes to the accounts, in so far as the information given above allows, for the following accounting items.
   (1) Share capital
   (2) Directors' remuneration   (60 mins)

(c) The directors of the company are unclear as to the nature of goodwill. They have asked you to define it.
   (4 mins)
   (80 mins)

195

WOODPECKER LIMITED
EXTENDED TRIAL BALANCE AS AT 31 MARCH 20X4

	Ledger balances DR £'000	Ledger balances CR £'000	Adjustments DR £'000	Adjustments CR £'000	Profit & Loss Account DR £'000	Profit & Loss Account CR £'000	Balance Sheet Balances DR £'000	Balance Sheet Balances CR £'000
Salaries and wages	1,468				1,468			
Salesmen's commission	102		4		106			
Motor expenses	72		6		78			
Sales		8,086				8,086		
Buildings (acc dep)		117		21				138
Fixtures and fittings (acc dep)		176		65				241
Motor vehicles (acc dep)		219		189				408
Office equipment (acc dep)		51		37				88
Investment revaluation reserve		150						150
Directors' pension contributions	15				15			
Advertising	67			11	56			
Stock	731		937	937	731	937	937	
Trade debtors	840						840	
Provision for doubtful debts		20		17				37
Goodwill	20						20	
Purchases	5,035				5,035			
Land and buildings (cost)	1,267						1,267	
Fixtures and fittings (cost)	632						632	
Motor vehicles (cost)	745						745	
Office equipment (cost)	194						194	
Investment property	800						800	
Depreciation (motor vehicles)			189		189			
Depreciation (fixtures and fittings)			65		65			
Depreciation (office equipment)			37		37			
Depreciation (buildings)			21		21			
Ordinary share capital		1,000						1,000
10% Preference share capital		300						300
Directors' fees	7				7			
Share premium		250						250
Light and heat	19		7		26			
Interim dividend	15				15			
Increase in provision for doubtful debt			17		17			
General expenses	227		28	21	234			
Insurance	45			7	38			
Profit and loss account		778						778
Accruals				45				45
Prepayments			39				39	
Cash in hand	3						3	
Cash at bank		139						139
Trade creditors		568						568
8% Debentures		450						450
Profit					885			885
	12,304	12,304	1,350	1,350	9,023	9,023	5,477	5,477

4 Tiny toys

You have just begun work as the assistant to the Financial Director of Tiny Toys Ltd, a company which buys and sells toys. Your predecessor prepared an extended trial balance for the year ending 31 December 20X3 prior to leaving. This includes the normal year-end adjustments. The Financial Director has asked you to review the trial balance in the light of some further information which may be relevant to the accounts. She has asked you to make any adjustments necessary before they are published.

The extended trial balance of Tiny Toys Ltd is set out on page 198.

The following information is provided.

(a)   An audit fee of £950 needs to be provided for.

(b)   The amount representing share capital and reserves in the extended trial balance consists of 100,000 25p shares. The first issue of 50,000 shares was at par, a subsequent issue of 50,000 shares being at a premium of 30p and this balance remains in its entirety in the share premium account. The remainder consists of the brought forward balance on the profit and loss reserve.

(c)   A decision has been made to use half of the share premium account to make a bonus issue of ordinary 25p shares. No entries have been made in the extended trial balance to reflect this issue.

(d)   The amounts for rates and the depreciation of buildings should be split 50:50 between administrative and distribution cost classifications.

(e)   Included in the salaries are directors' emoluments of £45,000 of which £25,000 should be classed as administrative costs, the remainder being distribution costs. Also included in the salaries figure is £5,000 of the salesmen's commission. The remainder of the salaries and wages should be split 60% administration and 40% distribution costs.

(f)   Eighty per cent of the depreciation charge for vehicles should be classified as a distribution cost, the remainder being an administrative cost. The office equipment depreciation should be classed as an administrative expense.

(g)   Of the light and heat costs, £1,000 should be classed as administrative costs, the remainder being distribution.

(h)   £6,000 of the total motor expense are distribution costs, the remainder being administrative.

(i)   General expenses should be classed as administrative expenditure.

(j)   A building costing £35,000, NBV £32,500 was sold for £37,500. The correct entries have been made in the buildings cost and depreciation accounts, as well as the bank account, but the profit figure does not appear to have been entered in the ETB profit and loss account.

(k)   On 1 December 20X3 there was an issue of 10,000 £1 nominal 12% debentures at par. The issue has been correctly accounted for but no interest has been accrued.

(l)   The coding on the suspense account entry for £150 indicates it is an amount owing for motor expenses.

(m)   There is no tax charge for the year.

TINY TOYS LIMITED
EXTENDED TRIAL BALANCE AS AT 31 DECEMBER 20X3

Folio Description	Ledger balances DR £	Ledger balances CR £	Adjustments DR £	Adjustments CR £	Profit & Loss Account DR £	Profit & Loss Account CR £	Balance Sheet Balances DR £	Balance Sheet Balances CR £
Sales		183,500				183,500		
Purchases	114,300				114,300			
Carriage outwards	3,100				3,100			
Motor expenses	6,600		150		6,750			
Rates	3,900			330	3,570			
Advertising	2,200				2,200			
Salaries and wages	75,000				75,000			
Debtors	38,900						38,900	
Creditors		17,000						17,000
Cash in hand	500						500	
Cash at bank	4,000						4,000	
Stock 01.01.X3	12,800		12,900	12,900	12,800	12,900	12,900	
Vehicles: cost	20,000						20,000	
depreciation		7,500		2,500				10,000
Office equipment: cost	4,000						4,000	
depreciation		1,000		500				1,500
Buildings: cost	40,000						40,000	
depreciation		8,000		4,000				12,000
General expenses	500				500			
Provision for doubtful debts		1,800		200				2,000
Increase in prov for doubtful debts			200		200			
Bad debt	1,000				1,000			
Depreciation: vehicles			2,500		2,500			
office equipment			500		500			
buildings			4,000		4,000			
Light and heat	1,700		150		1,850			
Loss						31,870	31,870	
Prepayment (rates)			330				330	
Accrual (light and heat)				150				150
Debentures		10,000						10,000
Share capital and reserves		94,700						94,700
Suspense		5,000		150				5,150
	328,500	328,500	20,730	20,730	228,270	228,270	152,500	152,500

Tasks

(a) Make any adjustments you feel necessary to the balances in the extended trial balance as a result of the matters set out in the information above. Set out your adjustments in the form of journal entries. (Ignore the effect of any adjustments on taxation.) (20 mins)

(b) Draft a profit and loss account for the year ended 31 December 20X3 and a balance sheet as at that date in a form suitable for publication using Format 1 in accordance with the Companies Act as supplemented by FRS 3 *Reporting financial performance*. (You are *not* required to prepare a statement of total recognised gains and losses or the reconciliation of movements in shareholders' funds required under FRS 3.) You should assume that all the information relates to continuing operations. (45 mins)

(c) You have been asked to comment briefly on the following.

(i) The constituents of the working capital of Tiny Toys Ltd (6 mins)
(ii) The profitability of Tiny Toys Ltd (4 mins)
(iii) The difference between cash flow and profitability (5 mins)

(80 mins)

5 Lawnderer

You have been asked to assist the directors of Lawnderer Ltd, a company that markets and distributes lawnmowers and other garden machinery, in the preparation of the financial statements for the year ended 30 September 20X5. The company employs a bookkeeper who is competent in some areas of financial accounting but has gaps in his knowledge which you are required to fill. He has already prepared the extended trial balance which is set out on page 201.

The following further information is provided by the bookkeeper.

(a) The company disposed of motor vehicles during the year. The cost of the vehicles of £491,000 and the accumulated depreciation of £368,000 are still included in the figures in the trial balance. The sale proceeds of £187,000 were credited to the sales account.

(b) Salesmen's commission of £52,000 relating to sales in the year has not been paid or charged as an expense in the figures in the trial balance.

(c) Interest on the 9% debentures has been included in the trial balance only for the first six months of the year.

(d) The tax charge for the year has been calculated at £843,000.

(e) A final dividend of 5 pence per share has yet to be provided for. The authorised and issued share capital of the company consists of shares with a nominal value of 25p.

(f) Goodwill is being written off on a straight-line basis over a period of 10 years, but no amortisation has yet been charged in the trial balance.

(g) The doubtful debts provision in the trial balance has not yet been adjusted for this year. The total doubtful debts provision required has been calculated at £115,000.

The directors of the company have also had a meeting with you regarding the possible treatment of certain future expenditure in the financial statements of the company. They have told you that the company has been approached by an inventor who has an idea to develop a revolutionary new lawnmower. The project looks technically feasible and preliminary marketing studies suggest a significant market for the product. Cost and revenue projections suggest that future profits should adequately cover the cost of development and have a beneficial effect on the future profitability of the company. The only problem the directors foresee is how to finance the operation to completion given the high level of borrowing already in the company. Their other concern is the effect that the expenditure on developing the new product will have on future profits, given that it will take some time between commencing the project and commercial production.

The directors have also asked you, at the same meeting, about the contents of the directors' report.

Tasks

(a)   (i)   Make any adjustments you feel to be necessary to the balances in the extended trial balance as a result of the matters set out in the further information given by the bookkeeper above. Set out your adjustments in the form of journal entries (narratives are not required).

        (ii)   Calculate the new retained profit which would result from these adjustments being made.

        (Ignore any effect of these adjustments on the tax charge for the year as given above.)

(b)   Draft a balance sheet for the year ended 30 September 20X5, in a form suitable for publication, using Format 1 in accordance with the Companies Act 1985.

(c)   Answer the following questions of the directors arising out of the further information given to you by them.

        (i)   How would the costs of developing the new lawnmower be reflected in the future results of the company?

        (ii)   What is 'gearing'? Would Lawnderer Ltd be considered to be a highly geared company and, if so, how might this affect the decision of a potential lender to lend money to the company?

(d)   The directors are also aware that a directors' report has to be produced with the financial statements. State *four* things that must appear in the directors' report, with a brief explanation of their nature.

(90 mins)

LAWNDERER LIMITED: EXTENDED TRIAL BALANCE 30 SEPTEMBER 20X5

Description	Trial balance Debit £'000	Trial balance Credit £'000	Adjustments Debit £'000	Adjustments Credit £'000	Profit and loss account Debit £'000	Profit and loss account Credit £'000	Balance sheet Debit £'000	Balance sheet Credit £'000
Depreciation: Land and buildings			18		18			
Fixtures and fittings			72		72			
Motor vehicles			298		298			
Office equipment			24		24			
Goodwill	360						360	
Accruals				102				102
Dividends	120				120			
Interest on debentures	153				153			
Net sales		22,129				22,129		
Trade debtors	2,603						2,603	
Prepayments			43				43	
Bank overdraft		362						362
Cash in hand	3						3	
Purchases	14,112				14,112			
Stock 1.10.X4	3,625				3,625			
Stock 30.9.X5			4,572	4,572		4,572	4,572	
Profit and loss account 1.10.X4		78						78
Provision for doubtful debts	134						134	
Trade creditors		2,967						2,967
Distribution costs	4,028		37	25	4,040			
9% Debentures		3,400						3,400
Administration expenses	1,736		65	18	1,783			
Accumulated depreciation: Land and buildings		83		18				101
Fixtures and fittings		214		72				286
Motor vehicles		644		298				942
Office equipment		83		24				107
Land and buildings (cost)	1,875						1,875	
Fixtures and fittings (cost)	576						576	
Motor vehicles (cost)	1,691						1,691	
Office equipment (cost)	244						244	
Called up share capital		1,000						1,000
Share premium		300						300
Profit					2,456			2,456
	31,260	31,260	5,129	5,129	26,701	26,701	12,101	12,101

Chapter 10 Cash flow statements

6 Bark

One of the partners in your firm of accountants has asked you to assist the accountant of Bark Ltd, a distributor of garden compost, in the production of a cash flow statement for the year ended 31 March 20X4. The financial statements of Bark Ltd, produced by the company's bookkeeper for internal purposes, are set out below, along with some further information relating to the reporting year.

BARK LIMITED
PROFIT AND LOSS ACCOUNT FOR THE YEAR ENDED 31 MARCH

	20X4		20X3	
	£'000	£'000	£'000	£'000
Turnover		3,845		3,335
Opening stock	523		445	
Purchases	2,553		2,291	
Closing stock	(634)		(523)	
Cost of sales		2,442		2,213
Gross profit		1,403		1,122
Depreciation		253		228
Other expenses		(446)		(395)
Profit on sale of fixed assets		35		21
Operating profit for the year		739		520
Interest payable		(66)		(86)
Profit before tax		673		434
Taxation on profit		(235)		(152)
Profit after tax		438		282
Ordinary dividend		(85)		(65)
Retained profit		353		217

BARK LIMITED
BALANCE SHEET AS AT 31 MARCH

	20X4	20X3
	£'000	£'000
Fixed assets	1,774	1,340
Current assets		
Stocks	634	523
Debtors	463	461
Cash	-	63
	1,097	1,047
Current liabilities		
Trade creditors	447	575
Dividends payable	85	65
Taxation	186	132
Bank overdraft	103	-
	821	772
Net current assets	276	275
Long-term loan	523	541
	1,527	1,074
Capital and reserves		
Called up share capital	600	500
Profit and loss account	927	574
	1,527	1,074

Further information is as follows.

(a)   Fixed assets costing £164,000 with accumulated depreciation of £98,000 were sold in the year for £101,000.

(b)   All sales and purchases were on credit. Other expenses were paid for in cash.

Tasks

(a)   Prepare a cash flow statement for Bark Ltd for the year ended 31 March 20X4 using the 'indirect method'. The revised FRS 1 format should be used.   (30 mins)

(b)   Provide a reconciliation between cash flows from operating activities and operating profit.   (15 mins)

(45 mins)

7 George

You have been given the following information about George Ltd for the year ending 31 March 20X5, with comparative figures for the year ending 31 March 20X4.

GEORGE LIMITED
PROFIT AND LOSS FOR THE YEAR ENDED 31 MARCH

	20X5		20X4	
	£'000	£'000	£'000	£'000
Turnover		2,500		1,775
Opening stock	200		100	
Purchases	1,500		1,000	
Closing stock	(210)		(200)	
Cost of sales		1,490		900
Gross profit		1,010		875
Depreciation		(275)		(250)
Other expenses		(500)		(425)
Profit on sales of fixed assets		2		-
Operating profit for the year		237		200
Interest paid		(20)		(35)
Profit before tax		217		165
Taxation on profit		(25)		(21)
Profit after tax		192		144
Proposed dividends		(35)		(30)
Retained profit		157		114

GEORGE LIMITED
BALANCE SHEET AS AT 31 MARCH

	20X5		20X4	
	£'000	£'000	£'000	£'000
Fixed assets		330		500
Current assets				
Stocks	210		200	
Debtors	390		250	
Cash	-		10	
	600		460	
Current liabilities				
Trade creditors	150		160	
Dividends payable	35		30	
Taxation	25		21	
Bank overdraft	199		-	
	409		211	
Net current assets		191		249
		521		749
Debentures				500
Long-term loan		200		100
		321		149

	20X5 £'000	20X4 £'000
Capital and reserves		
Called up share capital	40	25
Profit and loss account	281	124
	321	149

Further information

(a) In May 20X4 an asset was sold which originally cost £10,000 and was purchased when the company was started up two years ago. A new asset was bought for £110,000 in June 20X4. Fixed assets are depreciated at 25% of cost. The policy is to charge a full year's depreciation in the year of purchase and none in the year of sale.

(b) Loan interest is charged at 10% per annum. The long-term loan was increased on 1 April 20X4.

(c) The 5% debentures were redeemed on 1 April 20X4.

(d) Sales and purchases were on credit. All other expenses, including interest due, were paid in cash.

(e) On 1 October 20X4 there was a new issue of shares. Fifteen thousand ordinary £1 shares were issued at par.

Tasks

(a) Prepare a cash flow statement for the period.
(b) Prepare a reconciliation between cash flows from operating activities and operating profit.

(30 mins)

Chapter 11 Ratio analysis

8 Ratios

The following are the summarised accounts for Carrow Ltd, a company with an accounting year ending on 30 September.

SUMMARISED BALANCE SHEETS AS AT 30 SEPTEMBER

	20X6		20X7	
	£'000	£'000	£'000	£'000
Tangible fixed assets (at cost less depreciation)		4,995		12,700
Current assets				
Stocks	40,145		50,455	
Debtors	40,210		43,370	
Cash at bank	12,092		5,790	
	92,447		99,615	
Creditors: amounts falling due within one year				
Trade creditors	32,604		37,230	
Taxation	2,473		3,260	
Proposed dividend	1,785		1,985	
	36,862		42,475	
Net current assets		55,585		57,140
Total assets less current liabilities		60,580		69,840
Creditors: amounts falling due after more than one year				
10% debenture 2006/2010		19,840		19,840
		40,740		50,000
Capital and reserves				
Called-up share capital of £0.25 per share		9,920		9,920
Profit and loss account		30,820		40,080
		40,740		50,000

BPP
PROFESSIONAL EDUCATION

SUMMARISED PROFIT AND LOSS ACCOUNTS
FOR THE YEAR ENDED 30 SEPTEMBER

	20X6 £'000	20X7 £'000
Turnover	486,300	583,900
Operating profit	17,238	20,670
Interest payable	1,984	1,984
Profit on ordinary activities before taxation	15,254	18,686
Tax on profit on ordinary activities	5,734	7,026
Profit for the financial year	9,520	11,660
Dividends	2,240	2,400
Retained profit for the year	7,280	9,260
Retained profits brought forward	23,540	30,820
Retained profits carried forward	30,820	40,080

Task

Calculate, for each year, two ratios for each of the following user groups, which are of particular significance to them.

(a) Shareholders
(b) Trade creditors
(c) Internal management

Guidance notes

1 This tutorial question simply asks for calculations. In a central assessment you would almost certainly be asked to comment on any changes revealed by your ratios.

2 You should target your answer to the requirement of the question. For example, shareholders are unlikely to be particularly interested in the current or quick ratio.

3 Do not simply show numbers in your calculations; show in words how the ratio is calculated. Remember that there are sometimes different ways of calculating a ratio; if the assessor understands the method you have used, he is more likely to give you credit.

9 Ratio jargon

A managing director returns from a frustrating interview with the manager of the bank where the business has its account. He turns to you for advice stating:

'The bank manager told me that the working capital ratio is too low, and the gearing ratio too high. As far as I am concerned this is just meaningless jargon.'

Task

Briefly explain the bank manager's statement in words which the managing director will understand.

Guidance note

An important aspect of the accounting technician's role is to explain technical matters to the layman. This question should give you some practice.

Chapters 12 to 14 Group accounts

10 Bath

Bath Ltd acquired 80% of the ordinary share capital of Jankin Ltd on 1 January 20X1 for the sum of £153,000 and 60% of the ordinary share capital of Arthur Ltd on 1 July 20X1 for the sum of £504,000.

From the information given below you are required to prepare the consolidated balance sheet of Bath Ltd at 31 December 20X1.

Comparative figures, notes to the accounts and an auditor's report are not required.

Workings must be shown.

(a)   The balance sheets of the three companies at 31 December 20X1 are set out below.

	Bath Limited £	Jankin Limited £	Arthur Limited £
Share capital			
Ordinary shares of £0.25 each	750,000	100,000	400,000
Share premium	15,000	–	–
Profit and loss account			
1 January 20X1	191,000	19,400	132,000
Retained profits for 20X1	37,000	3,000	54,000
Taxation	78,000	24,000	56,000
Creditors	162,000	74,400	149,000
Bank overdraft: Bank A	74,000	–	–
Depreciation			
Freehold property	9,000	–	40,000
Plant and machinery	87,000	39,000	124,600
Dividends proposed	30,000	15,000	24,000
Current account	–	9,800	–
	1,433,000	284,600	979,600

	Bath Limited £	Jankin Limited £	Arthur Limited £
Freehold property, at cost	116,000	–	200,000
Plant and machinery, at cost	216,000	104,000	326,400
Investments in subsidiaries			
Jankin Limited	153,000	–	–
Arthur Limited	504,000	–	–
Trade investment	52,000	–	–
Stocks and work in progress	206,000	99,000	294,200
Debtors	172,200	73,000	95,000
Bank balance: Bank B	–	7,900	62,800
Cash	1,100	700	1,200
Current account	12,700	–	–
	1,433,000	284,600	979,600

(b) No interim dividends were declared or paid in 20X1 out of 20X1 profits. Bath Ltd has not yet accounted for dividends receivable from its subsidiary companies.

(c) A remittance of £1,700 from Jankin Ltd in December 20X1 was not received by Bath Ltd until January 20X2.

(d) An invoice for £1,200 for stock material (including £240 profit) had been included in sales in 20X1 by Bath Ltd but it was not received by Jankin Ltd until 20X2.

(e) In Jankin Ltd's stock at 31 December 20X1, were goods to the value of £8,000 ex Bath Ltd on which the latter had taken profit of £1,600.

(f) Profits of Arthur Ltd are deemed to have accrued equally throughout the year.

(g) Any goodwill arising on consolidation is to be amortised over four years.

(60 mins)

Lecturers'
Practice Exam

LECTURERS' PRACTICE EXAM

TECHNICIAN STAGE – NVQ4

Unit 11

Drafting Financial Statements
(Accounting Practice, Industry and Commerce)

Time allowed – 3 hours plus 15 minutes' reading time

BPP note

This exam has been amended to reflect the form and content of the new standards.

DO NOT OPEN THIS PAPER UNTIL YOU ARE READY TO START
UNDER TIMED CONDITIONS

Section 1

You are advised to spend approximately 125 minutes on this section.

This section is in three parts.

Part A

You should spend about 45 minutes on this part.

DATA

You have been asked to assist in the preparation of the consolidated accounts of the Shopan Group. Set out below on the balance sheets of Shopan Ltd and its subsidiary undertaking Hower Ltd, as at 30 September 20X9.

BALANCE SHEETS AS AT 30 SEPTEMBER 20X9

	Shopan Limited		Hower Limited	
	£'000	£'000	£'000	£'000
Fixed assets		6,273		1,633
Investment in Hower Ltd		2,100		
Current assets				
Stock	1,901		865	
Debtors	1,555		547	
Cash	184		104	
	3,640		1,516	
Current liabilities				
Trade creditors	1,516		457	
Taxation	431		188	
	1,947		645	
Net current assets		1,693		871
Long-term loan		(2,870)		(400)
		7,196		2,104
Capital and reserves		2,000		500
Called up share capital		950		120
Share premium		4,246		1,484
Profit and loss account		7,196		2,104

Further information

(a) The share capital of both Shopan Ltd and Hower Ltd consists of ordinary shares of £1 each.

(b) Shopan Ltd acquired 375,000 shares in Hower Ltd on 30 September 20X9.

(c) The fair value of the fixed assets of Hower Ltd at 30 September 20X9 was £2,033,000.

TASK 1.1

Prepare a consolidated balance sheet for Shopan Ltd and its subsidiary undertaking as at 30 September 20X9.

TASK 1.2

FRS 2 states that 'a parent undertaking should prepare consolidated financial statements for its group'. Give two of the criteria that, according to FRS 2, determine whether an undertaking is the parent undertaking of another undertaking.

Part B

You should spend about 50 minutes on this part.

DATA

You have been asked to help prepare the financial statements of Kettering plc for the year ended 31 March 20X1. The trial balance of the company as at 31 March 20X1 is set out below.

KETTERING PLC
TRIAL BALANCE AS AT 31 MARCH 20X1

	Debit £'000	Credit £'000
Accruals		540
Administrative expenses	5,404	
Buildings: cost	12,292	
Buildings: accumulated depreciation		1,680
Cash at bank	740	
Distribution costs	8,068	
Fixtures and fittings: cost	8,676	
Fixtures and fittings: accumulated depreciation		3,024
Interest	1,600	
Interim dividend	1,800	
Land: cost	20,600	
Long term loan		20,000
Motor vehicles: cost	18,436	
Motor vehicles: accumulated depreciation		8,056
Office equipment: cost	3,708	
Office equipment: accumulated depreciation		1,528
Ordinary share capital		12,000
Prepayments	368	
Profit and loss account		21,360
Provision for doubtful debts		428
Purchases	55,364	
Sales		85,532
Share premium		6,000
Stock as at 1 April 20X0	18,064	
Trade creditors		9,228
Trade debtors	14,256	
	169,376	169,376

Further information

(a)   The authorised share capital of the company, all of which has been issued, consists of ordinary shares with a nominal value of £1.

(b)   The company paid an interim dividend of 15p per share during the year but has not provided for the proposed final dividend of 10p per share.

(c)   Additions to fixed assets were:

Motor vehicles   £5,360
Office equipment   £1,072

Motor vehicles which had cost £3,900,000 and which had accumulated depreciation of £2,024,000 were disposed of during the year. There were no other additions or disposals. All of the additions and disposals have been included in the accounts as at 31 March 20X1.

(d)   The stock at the close of business on 31 March 20X1 was valued at cost at £21,384.

(e)   The corporation tax charge for the year has been calculated as £5,892,000.

(f)   No depreciation charges for the year have been entered into the accounts as at 31 March 20X1. The depreciation charges for the year are as follows.

	£'000
Buildings	260
Fixtures and fittings	868
Motor vehicles	2,592
Office equipment	740

(g)   The land has been revalued by professional valuers at £24,000,000. The revaluation is to be included in the financial statements for the year ended 31 March 20X1.

(h)   Legal proceedings have been started against Kettering Ltd because of faulty products supplied to a customer. The company's lawyers advise that it is probable that the entity will be found liable for damages of £1,000,000.

TASK 1.3

Make the necessary journal entries as a result of the further information given above. Dates and narratives are not required.

Notes

(a)   You must show any workings relevant to these adjustments.
(b)   Ignore any effect of these adjustments on the tax charge for the year given above.

TASK 1.4

Draft a note to the accounts showing movements on tangible fixed assets, as far as the information given allows.

TASK 1.5

Explain your treatment of the probable damages arising from the legal proceedings. Refer, where relevant, to accounting standards.

Part C

You should spend about 30 minutes on this part.

DATA

A colleague has asked you to take over the drafting of a cash flow statement for Diewelt Ltd for the year ended 30 September 20X9. Your colleague has already drafted a reconciliation between cash flows from operating activities and operating profit for the period. The financial statements of the company, drafted for internal purposes, along with the reconciliation are set out below, together with some further information relating to the reporting year.

DIEWELT LIMITED
PROFIT AND LOSS ACCOUNT FOR THE YEAR ENDED SEPTEMBER 20X9

	20X9
	£'000
Turnover	9,804
Cost of sales	5,784
Gross profit	4,020
Profit on sale of fixed asset	57
Depreciation	985
Other expenses	819
Operating profit for the year	2,273
Interest paid	365
Profit before tax	1,908
Taxation on profit	583
Profit after tax	1,325
Ordinary dividend	440
Retained profit	885

DIEWELT LIMITED
BALANCE SHEET AS AT 30 SEPTEMBER 20X9

	20X9		20X8	
	£'000	£'000	£'000	£'000
Fixed assets		6,490		5,620
Current assets				
Stock	3,151		2,106	
Trade debtors	2,314		1,470	
Cash	103		383	
	5,568		3,959	
Current liabilities				
Trade creditors	964		1,034	
Dividends payable	264		192	
Taxation	583		491	
	1,811		1,717	
Net current assets		3,757		2,242
Long-term loan		(3,300)		(2,900)
		6,947		4,962
Capital and reserves		2,200		1,600
Called up share capital		800		300
Profit and loss account		3,947		3,062
		6,947		4,962

Further information

(a) A fixed asset which had cost £136,000 and had accumulated depreciation of £85,000 was sold during the year.

(b) All sales and purchases were on credit. Other expenses were paid for in cash.

RECONCILIATION OF OPERATING PROFIT
TO NET CASH INFLOW FROM OPERATING ACTIVITIES

	£'000
Operating profit	2,273
Depreciation charges	985
Profit on sale of tangible fixed assets	(57)
Increase in stock	(1,045)
Increase in debtors	(844)
Decrease in creditors	(70)
Net cash inflow from operating activities	1,242

TASK 1.6

Prepare a cash flow statement for Diewelt Ltd for the year ended 30 September 20X9 in accordance with the requirements of FRS 1 (Revised).

Section 2

You are advised to spend approximately 55 minutes on this section.

This section is in two parts.

Part A

You should spend about 40 minutes on this part.

DATA

Jonathan Fisher is intending to invest a substantial sum of money in a company. A colleague has suggested to him that he might want to invest in a private company called Carp Ltd which supplies pond equipment to retail outlets. You have been asked to assist him in interpreting the financial statements of the company which are set out below.

CARP LIMITED
SUMMARY PROFIT AND LOSS ACCOUNT FOR THE YEAR ENDED 30 SEPTEMBER

	20X9	20X8
	£'000	£'000
Turnover	3,183	2,756
Cost of sales	1,337	1,020
Gross profit	1,846	1,736
Expenses	1,178	1,047
Net profit before interest and tax	668	689
Interest	225	92
Profit before tax	443	597
Taxation	87	126
Profit after tax	356	471
Dividends	42	50
Retained profit	314	421

CARP LIMITED
SUMMARY BALANCE SHEETS AS AT 30 SEPTEMBER

	20X9		20X8	
	£'000	£'000	£'000	£'000
Fixed assets		4,214		2,030
Current assets				
Stock	795		689	
Debtors	531		459	
Cash	15		136	
	1,341		1,284	
Current liabilities				
Trade creditors	709		435	
Proposed dividend	42		50	
Taxation	87		126	
	838		611	
Net current assets		503		673
Long-term loan		(2,500)		(1,000)
		2,217		1,703
Share capital		700		500
Profit and loss account		1,517		1,203
		2,217		1,703

TASK 2.1

Prepare notes for Jonathan Fisher covering the following points.

(a) Explain what a 'balance sheet' is and what a 'profit and loss account' is and identify the elements that appear in each statement.

(b) Explain the 'accounting equation' and demonstrate that the balance sheet of Carp Ltd as at 30 September 20X9 conforms to it.

(c) Calculate the following ratios for the two years.

    (i)   Gearing
    (ii)   Net profit percentage
    (iii)   Current ratio
    (iv)   Return on equity

(d) Using the ratios calculated, comment on the company's profitability, liquidity and financial position and consider how these have changed over the two years.

(e) Using only the calculation of the ratios and the analysis of the changes over the two years, state whether the company is a better prospect for investment in 20X9 than it was in 20X8. Give reasons for your answer.

Part B

You should spend about 15 minutes on this part.

TASK 2.2

The Accounting Standards Board's *Statement of Principles for Financial Reporting* states that:

'The objective of financial statements is to provide information about the reporting entity's financial performance and financial position that is useful to a wide range of users for assessing the stewardship of management and for making economic decisions.'

Illustrate this objective by:

(a)   Selecting one external user of limited company financial statements and showing how it uses financial statements to assess the stewardship of management

(b)   Selecting one external user of limited company financial statements and showing how it uses financial statements to make economic decisions

See overleaf for information on other
BPP products and how to order

AAT Order

To BPP Professional Education, Aldine Place, London W12 8AW

Tel: 020 8740 2211. Fax: 020 8740 1184

E-mail: Publishing@bpp.com Web:www.bpp.com

Mr/Mrs/Ms (Full name)

Daytime delivery address

Postcode

Daytime Tel

E-mail

	5/03 Texts	5/03 Kits	Special offer	8/03 Passcards	Tapes
FOUNDATION (£14.95 except as indicated)				Foundation	
Units 1 & 2 Receipts and Payments	☐	☐	Foundation Sage Bookeeping and Excel Spreadsheets CD-ROM free if ordering all Foundation Text and Kits, including Units 21 and 22/23 ☐	£6.95 ☐	£10.00 ☐
Unit 3 Ledger Balances and Initial Trial Balance	☐	☐			
Unit 4 Supplying Information for Mgmt Control	☐				
Unit 21 Working with Computers (£9.95) (6/03)	☐				
Unit 22/23 Healthy Workplace/Personal Effectiveness (£9.95)	☐				
Sage and Excel for Foundation (CD-ROM £9.95)	☐				
INTERMEDIATE (£9.95 except as indicated)					
Unit 5 Financial Records and Accounts	☐	☐		£5.95 ☐	£10.00 ☐
Unit 6/7 Costs and Reports (Combined Text £14.95)	☐				
Unit 6 Costs and Revenues	☐	☐		£5.95 ☐	£10.00 ☐
Unit 7 Reports and Returns	☐	☐		£5.95 ☐	
TECHNICIAN (£9.95 except as indicated)					
Unit 8/9 Managing Performance and Controlling Resources	☐	☐		£5.95 ☐	£10.00 ☐
Spreadsheets for Technician (CD-ROM)	☐		Spreadsheets for Technicians CD-ROM free if take Unit 8/9 Text and Kit ☐		
Unit 10 Core Managing Systems and People (£14.95)	☐	☐		£5.95 ☐	£10.00 ☐
Unit 11 Option Financial Statements (A/c Practice)	☐	☐		£5.95 ☐	
Unit 12 Option Financial Statements (Central Govnmt)	☐	☐		£5.95 ☐	
Unit 15 Option Cash Management and Credit Control	☐	☐		£5.95 ☐	
Unit 17 Option Implementing Audit Procedures	☐	☐			
Unit 18 Option Business Tax (FA03)(8/03 Text & Kit)	☐	☐			
Unit 19 Option Personal Tax (FA 03)(8/03 Text & Kit)	☐	☐			
TECHNICIAN 2002 (£9.95)					
Unit 18 Option Business Tax FA02 (8/02 Text & Kit)	☐	☐			
Unit 19 Option Personal Tax FA02 (8/02 Text & Kit)	☐	☐			
SUBTOTAL	£	£	£	£	£

TOTAL FOR PRODUCTS £

POSTAGE & PACKING

Texts/Kits	First	Each extra
UK	£3.00	£3.00 £
Europe*	£6.00	£4.00 £
Rest of world	£20.00	£10.00 £
Passcards		
UK	£2.00	£1.00 £
Europe*	£3.00	£2.00 £
Rest of world	£8.00	£8.00 £
Tapes		
UK	£2.00	£1.00 £
Europe*	£3.00	£2.00 £
Rest of world	£8.00	£8.00 £

TOTAL FOR POSTAGE & PACKING £

(Max £12 Texts/Kits/Passcards - deliveries in UK)

Grand Total (Cheques to *BPP Professional Education*)

I enclose a cheque for (incl. Postage) £

Or charge to Access/Visa/Switch

Card Number

Expiry date   Start Date

Issue Number (Switch Only)

Signature

We aim to deliver to all UK addresses inside 5 working days; a signature will be required. Orders to all EU addresses should be delivered within 6 working days. All other orders to overseas addresses should be delivered within 8 working days. * Europe includes the Republic of Ireland and the Channel Islands.

See overleaf for information on other
BPP products and how to order

AAT Order

To BPP Professional Education, Aldine Place, London W12 8AW
Tel: 020 8740 2211. Fax: 020 8740 1184
E-mail: Publishing@bpp.com Web:www.bpp.com

Mr/Mrs/Ms (Full name)

Daytime delivery address

Postcode

Daytime Tel   E-mail

OTHER MATERIAL FOR AAT STUDENTS	8/03 Texts	3/03 Text
FOUNDATION (£5.95)		
Basic Mathematics	☐	
INTERMEDIATE (£5.95)		
Basic Bookkeeping (for students exempt from Foundation)	☐	
FOR ALL STUDENTS (£5.95)		
Building Your Portfolio (old standards)		☐
Building Your Portfolio (new standards)	☐	

£ ☐   £ ☐

TOTAL FOR PRODUCTS £ ☐

POSTAGE & PACKING

Texts/Kits	First	Each extra	
UK	£3.00	£3.00	£ ☐
Europe*	£6.00	£4.00	£ ☐
Rest of world	£20.00	£10.00	£ ☐
Passcards			
UK	£2.00	£1.00	£ ☐
Europe*	£3.00	£2.00	£ ☐
Rest of world	£8.00	£8.00	£ ☐
Tapes			
UK	£2.00	£1.00	£ ☐
Europe*	£3.00	£2.00	£ ☐
Rest of world	£8.00	£8.00	£ ☐

TOTAL FOR POSTAGE & PACKING £ ☐
(Max £12 Texts/Kits/Passcards - deliveries in UK)

Grand Total (Cheques to *BPP Professional Education*)
I enclose a cheque for (incl. Postage) **£** ☐
Or charge to Access/Visa/Switch
Card Number ☐☐☐☐☐☐☐☐☐☐☐☐☐☐☐☐

Expiry date ☐☐☐☐   Start Date

Issue Number (Switch Only)

Signature

Review Form & Free Prize Draw – Unit 11 Drafting Financial Statements

All original review forms from the entire BPP range, completed with genuine comments, will be entered into one of two draws on 31 January 2004 and 31 July 2004. The names on the first four forms picked out on each occasion will be sent a cheque for £50.

Name: _____   Address: _____

_____

_____

How have you used this Assessment Kit?
(Tick one box only)

☐ Home study (book only)

☐ On a course: college _____

☐ With 'correspondence' package

☐ Other _____

Why did you decide to purchase this Assessment Kit? *(Tick one box only)*

☐ Have used BPP Texts in the past

☐ Recommendation by friend/colleague

☐ Recommendation by a lecturer at college

☐ Saw advertising

☐ Other _____

During the past six months do you recall seeing/receiving any of the following?
(Tick as many boxes as are relevant)

☐ Our advertisement in *Accounting Technician* magazine

☐ Our advertisement in *Pass*

☐ Our brochure with a letter through the post

Which (if any) aspects of our advertising do you find useful?
(Tick as many boxes as are relevant)

☐ Prices and publication dates of new editions

☐ Information on Assessment Kit content

☐ Facility to order books off-the-page

☐ None of the above

Have you used the companion Interactive Text for this subject?   ☐ Yes   ☐ No

Your ratings, comments and suggestions would be appreciated on the following areas

	Very useful	Useful	Not useful
Practice Activities	☐	☐	☐
Full exam based assessments	☐	☐	☐
Specimen exam	☐	☐	☐

	Excellent	Good	Adequate	Poor
Overall opinion of this Kit	☐	☐	☐	☐

Do you intend to continue using BPP Interactive Texts/Assessment Kits?   ☐ Yes   ☐ No

Please note any further comments and suggestions/errors on the reverse of this page.

The BPP author of this edition can be e-mailed at: katyhibbert@bpp.com

Review Form & Free Prize Draw (continued)

Please note any further comments and suggestions/errors below

Free Prize Draw Rules

1   Closing date for 31 January 2004 draw is 31 December 2003. Closing date for 31 July 2004 draw is 30 June 2004.

2   Restricted to entries with UK and Eire addresses only. BPP employees, their families and business associates are excluded.

3   No purchase necessary. Entry forms are available upon request from BPP Professional Education. No more than one entry per title, per person. Draw restricted to persons aged 16 and over.

4   Winners will be notified by post and receive their cheques not later than 6 weeks after the relevant draw date.

5   The decision of the promoter in all matters is final and binding. No correspondence will be entered into.